More than Chance

When God is the only logical explanation

ANDREW KEITH SMITH

CONTENTS

DEDICATION

This book is dedicated to my children, Christopher, Jennifer, Joanna and Stephen, who, when younger, did not always fully understand why I did what I did, but still loved me as I loved them. Putting some of my thoughts and experiences into print helps me to explain my motivation and actions over many years. But like any other frail human being I realize that I did not always get it right – that's why I needed, and still need, the continual input of God the Holy Spirit who enables us to do extraordinary exploits.

FORWORD

Whenever something wonderful happens in a person's life, there are many ways of communicating it so others may share the joy. The gospel of Jesus Christ is no exception, as there are literally hundreds of ways to pass on the good news of the Kingdom. However, one of the most effective tools we have is our own story of God's interaction in our own lives. What you have in these pages before you is precisely that: a testimony that reveals one man's life journey, how God shaped and fine-tuned that journey, and through which the Lord revealed His own identity and character.

I met Andrew Smith at Kings Cross Baptist Church in 2013, just a few months after my arrival in the UK. My intention was to familiarise myself with this reportedly influential church in central London, but on that day I found more than merely a pastor; I found a beloved friend and a faithful Kingdom partner.

Our affinity blossomed upon discovering our common roots in the African continent. Andrew spent many of his years in South Africa; my wife Judy (the granddaughter of an African missionary who first set foot on African soil in 1917) was born in Belgian Congo, and we spent a year there serving the Lord in 1985. Andrew and I also discovered a common passion for whole-church evangelism and disciple making, and I quickly came to realise this man's keen focus on the Great Commission. Words fail to express my appreciation for Andrew's investment in my life and the multitude of people to whom he has introduced me throughout the city.

What has amazed me most of all about Andrew was reading this story and seeing the hand of God in his life over many formative years. His life was marked with numerous confusing crossroads, and like all of us, he sometimes made mistakes. However, he has maintained a faith and vision for the Kingdom that few people sustain over so many years, and the result is a man of God who stands strong in Christ and stubbornly resists retirement from what has truly been the adventure of a lifetime.

As you read this anthology of personal anecdotes and life lessons, it is my prayer that you will see and experience God in a fresh, new way. Listen to His voice, not only from the Word of God, but from the testimony of how this man put the Word into action along each step of the journey. Most of all, I dearly desire that you take courage to step out in faith—to get on board with the work of the unfinished task that lies before us, that you will know through obedient service the depth of joy that few of us dare to fully discover for ourselves.

Ben Armacost founder of the AIM Trainers network (aimtrainers.org) author of *Bridge to the Beautiful City*

London, England October 2016

CHAPTER ONE

Where He leads me I will follow

Travelling out of Johannesburg by car, on the highway which leads to the international airport, I began to think about a couple who lived in a suburb quite close to the road. I had not seen Marcel and Suzette for a number years, they were members of the first church that I attended in Johannesburg when I arrived there as a young man at the end of 1967. It was the mid eighties, and I was the pastor of a small church which I had planted on the outskirts of the city. The church could not pay me so I worked for a small business as a company representative. That morning, I was heading for the industrial area to keep an appointment for 10.30am.

Once I started thinking about Marcel and Suzette, I could not get them out of my mind. They had been parental figures for the young adults of the church, encouraging us in our faith, and generally being a blessing in those far off days. But, on the road that day, I got the very strong impression that God wanted me to go and visit them immediately. I started discussing my options with the Lord, out loud. I told Him that I could not go immediately as I had an appointment at 10.30am, which needed to be kept. However, I assured Him that I would go right after I had finished my business. This I did, arriving at their house at about midday.

I knocked at the front door and Suzette answered my knock. She looked pleased to see me and said what a surprise it was to have the visit. She asked me what had prompted my call, so I tried to explain how God had spoken to me while I was driving along the highway, giving me the strong impression that I needed to speak to Marcel right away if possible. Suzette looked a little taken back and then burst into tears. I asked her what the problem was, and she began to tell me how Marcel had decided to close his business as it was no longer viable. That morning he had been on the phone in the sitting room, putting off his customers, while she had been sitting the other side of the room praying, asking God to send someone to help him in his difficult time.

Now of course you know the rest of the story. While Suzette was talking to the Lord, asking Him to send someone to encourage Marcel, I was driving along the highway telling the Lord that I could not go immediately because I had an appointment at 10.30am. For that reason I did not get there until midday, and Marcel had already gone into the office to sort out the closing of his business. Thankfully, when Suzette phoned him, he was able to return home. We spent time together discussing the implications of his difficult experience, and we prayed for God's inspiration to understand what He was saying to Marcel, so that he could put his life back on track. I have no doubt that our time together was a blessing, because God organized it in the first place.

The question is, how on earth did that happen? If God is just a delusion, as Richard Dawkins would have us believe, how did Suzette's prayers penetrate my mind while I was driving down the highway and so profoundly affect me that I felt compelled to visit them? It was not as if she was praying about me in particular, as we had not seen each other for a long time. Besides that, how come I just happened to be passing their suburb at just the right time, on the day that I was needed? There are those who would put it all down to chance, but I am sure that such occurrences are more than chance or coincidence. I believe in a God who is able to deliver me from evil, save me from sin, and empower me to live a life which is a blessing to my fellow human beings.

All I need to do is receive His salvation through Jesus and make Him the Lord of my life, which means that I will continually seek His guidance and follow His teaching on a day to day basis. Salvation is not just a free ticket to Heaven- it is a way of life!

In the western world today a number of prominent individuals passionately believe that there is no God, and they are evangelical in their fervour to make converts. They ridicule any form of monotheism, particularly Christianity, believing religion to be a crutch for the weak and the foolish. Their view of life is that everything that exists came into being by mere chance, and given enough time, something can evolve from nothing. One of the leading lights in this group is the scientist Richard Dawkins, who wrote the much publicised book, *The God Delusion*. Thankfully there have been a number of excellent books written in response to Richard Dawkins' publication, for example, Lee Strobel's book *The Case for a Creator*. In his book he presents the reader with a large amount of evidence to prove that the universe was intelligently designed, and he asks many questions of the evolutionary theory, to which the evolutionist has no answer. I am deeply grateful for his work and the work of other Christian writers, who skilfully and convincingly oppose those who propagate atheism.

However, it is important for us to recognize that we can neither prove nor disprove the existence of God scientifically, but we can prove God by faith. In fact the Bible challenges us to do just that. In Hebrews 11:6 the writer says:

> "And without faith it is impossible to please God, because anyone who comes to Him must believe that He exists and that He rewards those who earnestly seek Him." (NIV)

In other words, it is our faith in His existence, and our firm belief that He desires to be a blessing to those who receive His salvation, that enables us to experience His life, purpose and direction. Hebrews chapter 11 is full of illustrations about those in the Old Testament who took God at His word and trusted Him to do what He had promised, and God came through for them, often miraculously, proving His existence and working out His purpose in their lives. With the coming of Jesus the Son of God, in the New Testament, God's salvation is made perfect. Those who believe in Him are filled with the Holy Spirit who equips them to do God's will and accomplish His purpose. The book of Acts is an extraordinary record of what God was able to do through the early Church as people put their faith in Jesus' salvation and lived their lives for Him. Things happened that cannot be explained as random chance, and miracles occurred that have no scientific explanation.

The question is, has anything changed? Does God still defy science to miraculously accomplish His purpose through those who give their lives to Him? In my experience He does. Looking back at my life, I can recall many occasions when God did extraordinary things in and through us, and for us, so that His purpose would be accomplished. Some of these occurrences can be explained away scientifically; in other words, we can see how they happened, but we still recognize that it is God who arranged the circumstances to accomplish His purpose. However, on other occasions there is no scientific explanation, the only explanation is that God defied science to accomplish His purpose. Most often these things happened as a result of our prayers, or the prayers of others. Very often God worked when we, or others in our sphere of influence, were in real need, with our backs against the wall and no way out but God. If I have a plan B, just in case God does not come up with the solution, the chances are that He won't. But if God is my only option, and I have no other way out, then God acts on my behalf. He wants us to depend on Him alone.

CHAPTER TWO

Starting out

I had the privilege of growing up in a missionary home in Zambia, in southern Africa, at that time known by its colonial name, Northern Rhodesia. My Father received his call to missions while serving with the British armed forces in India in the 2nd world war. He was sitting on a packed train which had stopped at a station, and he was absolutely overcome by the teeming multitudes of people. His Bible was randomly open on his lap, and looking down at it he read from Mt. 9:37 & 38:

> "The harvest is plentiful but the workers are few. Ask the Lord of the harvest, therefore, to send out workers into the harvest field." (NIV)

Telling me the story years later he said, "Andrew, I just told the Lord that I would go, I would be a missionary."

I think Dad's first intention was to return to India after the war, but God obviously had other ideas, and the opportunities, when they came, were in Southern Rhodesia. So in 1949 my father and mother took their family of three small boys (I was just eighteen months old at the time) by ship to South Africa, and then by train to Southern Rhodesia, now Zimbabwe. Dad was an independent missionary, so for the first twelve years he worked in commerce to support the family and planted churches at the same time. We only stayed in Southern Rhodesia for about two and a half years and then moved up to Ndola in Northern Rhodesia, now Zambia.

It is not my intention to write my autobiography so I will not fill in the details, sufficient to say that the town of Ndola became my home, that is, where I spent my formative years.

When people ask me where I come from, I usually say Zambia. Ndola is also where I made my first commitment to Jesus and where God began to show me His extraordinary purpose for my life. My Father planted a number of churches in Ndola and in the surrounding towns. From the outset he worked with the Baptist Church, and after twelve years became a full time missionary. He went on to work in full time ministry until he was seventy-eight and continued to work part time until he was eighty-three. He truly was an inspiration to me.

We always lived very frugally, even when my father was working for a secular business to support the family. We had a nice car because it was provided by his secular employer, but only just enough of everything else to live on. It was years later that I discovered that a lot of my Father's earnings went into the mission, often to pay his pastors and evangelists. In fact most of their lives my Mom and Dad gave away much of what they had, but God always provided and protected. Quite early on in our time in Ndola, we lived just outside the main town in a place called the Health Department. I never quite found out what Dad did there, but he seemed to be away for quite a lot of the time. The house stood on its own with little protection from natural dangers. Parts of the building were only partially finished. The main bedroom was not decorated and had a pile of building material in the middle of the room, and no glass in the windows. My mother always kept the door locked so that we could not go into the room, nor could outsiders get into the rest of the house.

One evening, after the sun had gone down, there was a roaring sound, and to our horror we realised that there were lions outside knocking over the dustbins. Lions seldom came near to Ndola, but at the time there had been some other sightings. Fortunately we were safely locked inside and not really in danger. However, there was another incident which was far more dangerous. My father was away, so my mother was on her own with three small boys and a new baby. A huge fire was advancing towards the house consuming the one-and-a-half metre high elephant grass as it came towards us. We had a narrow fire break behind the house just a few metres wide. Mom gathered us together and prayed that the Lord would protect us, which He undoubtedly did. The following day we went outside to look at the damage. The fire had devastated everything around us, but the house was untouched. We found a number of dead animals including a calf and a cat. I gave the body of the cat a push with the toe of my shoe, and discovered to my surprise that this mother cat had been protecting her kittens. Sadly all of them were dead except for one, which crawled out from under its mother's burnt body. Its only injury was that it had lost its tail in the fire. We took him home and named him Smoky. He survived, and over time his tail grew back at a strange angle. This incident always reminds me of our Lord's cry of anguish over Jerusalem in Mt.23:37:

> "O Jerusalem, Jerusalem, you who kill the prophets and stone those sent to you, how often I have longed to gather your children together, as a hen gathers her chicks under her wings, but you were not willing."
> (NIV)

The Lord longs for us to put ourselves under His protection, but many do not believe and are consequently not interested in His wonderful offer of salvation. But there is no doubt that the Lord protects those who belong to Him. I know he has protected our family on many occasions of which we were aware, and on many other occasions when we were completely oblivious to the danger around us, and I am so grateful.

CHAPTER THREE

Moving south

I left school without university entrance – it was not that I was badly behaved, or lacking in ability, I just found it so difficult to pay attention. My father got me a job as a trainee at a local engineering business which had its head office in South Africa. I had been working there for about a year when the head office sent some of their staff to visit our branch in Ndola. Officially they were there to see how things were going and to encourage the local branch, but, on the quiet, they were offering jobs in South Africa to some of the local young men. I too was offered a job, and found the whole prospect rather exciting. I asked my father what he thought of the opportunity and he responded by asking me if I had prayed about it. He went on to say that I was eighteen, and if I felt the Lord wanted me to go, I could go. I was frankly amazed at how easy he had made it for me. I can't remember how much I prayed, but I knew I wanted to go, so I gave the South Africans a positive reply and very soon found myself on a train travelling south.

I arrived in a town called Vereeniging in January 1966. My new South African home was flat, industrial and polluted. Fortunately it had a good Baptist Church and a pastor who befriended me. I think my Dad had contacted him and encouraged him to "take me under his wing." Within a short time I was helping in the youth department and generally involving myself in the church. One day after work in the evening, I was in my room at my place of residence, when there was a knock at the door, and to my surprise it was an unscheduled visit from my pastor. He asked me if we could have a chat, and I readily agreed. He had just come back from a visit to the Baptist Theological College in Johannesburg, where he himself had trained for ministry. He told me that while he was there, God had spoken to him, and the word that he had received from the Lord was for me. In essence, God had told him to tell me that He wanted me to go to Bible College to train for the ministry. He felt that the message was of such importance that he did not go home, but came straight to my room to let me know what God had said to him.

I was rather taken aback by what he said. I thanked him but did not elaborate on my feelings at the time. From a young age I had thought that one day I would be a preacher, but I did not have the courage to tell anyone about my aspirations. My rather poor school results had left me with low self esteem, and I had little faith in my academic ability. I was reasonably certain that I was not capable of making it through a theological college course successfully, so I kept my thoughts about being a preacher to myself. However, hearing my pastor say that God had told him to encourage me to train for Christian ministry kindled a new interest within me. I was only 19 at the time, young and impressionable. But I am eternally grateful that he came and spoke to me when he did, because it helped me to understand that it was possibly not just my idea, or even my pastor's idea, maybe it was God's idea, and that made all the difference.

I only lasted two years in Vereeniging. The church was good, the pastor was a blessing, but I desperately wanted to live in a big city and Johannesburg was just forty miles up the road. I managed to organize a transfer, and God arranged another good church for me. I very soon became involved in the ministry of that church, just as I had been involved in the ministry of my church in Vereeniging. It was about that time that I realised that one of my gifts was that I could talk, so I left structural engineering and went into retail. It was not that I intended making that my career, it was just a more pleasant way of supporting myself while I worked out how I was going to further my education.

By the end of 1968 I had a plan. I would move to England, where I could complete my school education and apply for university entrance. I always took my annual holiday over Christmas so that I could go home to Ndola and be with my family. 1968 was no different, except I presumed that this trip would be my last trip home for a little while. I took my car to the local garage and asked the owner if he would give it a good service and hold on to it until I returned in three weeks. My plan was to sell it when I got back and to use the money to buy my ticket to England. I had already given my employer notice of my intention to stop work, so after saying farewell to my friends I began the very long trip home. My mode of transport was to stand beside the road and thumb a lift, commonly known as "hitch hiking." The trip from Johannesburg to Ndola took me approximately three days and two nights, sometimes less if I got good lifts. In those days it was safer than it is today, but there was still a certain amount of risk involved. Thankfully the Lord always looked after me! I had a great time with my family and got back to Johannesburg three weeks later.

Upon return, one of the first things I did was to go to the garage to pick up my car. I wanted to get it sold as soon as possible. However, when the garage owner caught sight of me he looked as if he had something difficult to tell me. I asked him if everything was alright and he said that there had been a problem. Apparently, while I was away he had found it difficult to keep my car inside all the time, so he had left it outside during the day. Unfortunately a big American car had come around the corner and smashed into my car. Fortunately the garage owner had caught the driver who had promised to pay for my cars extensive repairs. To say the least, I was a bit shocked. I did not have that much time and

I had no income. I had hoped to sell the car quickly and move on.

That evening, at supper, a friend asked if I would like to go out and see a film in the city to take my mind of things. I agreed, and we set out in his car. He had a particular film that he wanted to see, but when we arrived at the cinema we discovered that we had the wrong venue, so he turned the car around and went back the way we had come. We had just gone through a junction with traffic lights, when we saw another car coming straight for us on the wrong side of the road. Unfortunately there had been a minor accident involving a motorcycle which the rider had left in the middle of the road. The driver of the oncoming car only noticed the motorcycle at the last moment and swerved wildly to avoid it; as a result he hit us head on. Those were the days of no seat belts, and I, being a front seat passenger, went head first through the windscreen and then fell back onto my seat.

The accident occurred in the city centre and it was obviously serious, so a crowd gathered very quickly. Apparently I was more badly injured than anyone else in either car. My friend had an injury to his leg, but the steering wheel saved him from the windscreen. Somehow, onlookers got me out of the car and put me on the pavement. Despite receiving serious injuries, which included a fractured skull, a break on each side of my jaw, two ruptured ear drums and extensive lacerations to my face, I was still conscious. Sitting on the pavement edge I looked down into an ever growing pool of blood which was coming out of my nose, mouth, ears and the cuts in my face. My immediate thought was that I was going to die. But as soon as that thought came to me, it was interrupted by what I can only describe as a word from the Lord: "No you are not going to die, I have work for you to do." It was not an audible voice, but I knew that God was speaking to me.

The ambulance soon arrived and took us to the accident and emergency department of the city centre hospital. There are advantages to going into an unconscious state, the most important one being that you do not feel the pain. But as I have already mentioned, I did not have this protection. Before they stitched me up, they injected me five times in the face which was exceedingly painful. Once they had finished putting me back together again, I was taken to the motor accident ward. The hospital was attached to a university, so if you were an interesting case – and apparently I was – you had lectures about your injuries with the lecturer and students gathered around your bed. You could hear exactly what was wrong with you, in graphic detail.

After about a week, a lecturer and his students gathered around my bed. He started by saying, "We need to talk about this case while we still have the chance, because this young man is healing so fast he will soon be out of here." He then went on to describe the difference between a compressive fracture and a whiplash fracture to the skull. Apparently with a whiplash fracture, the injured individual always goes into an unconscious state and often lapses into a coma. This is due to the build up of cerebral fluid in the cranium and the resultant pressure on the brain. However, with a compressive fracture there is a chance in a million that the cerebral fluid will find a way of escape, and as a result the person will not go into an unconscious state; according to the lecturer I was that one in a million case. My ear drums had both ruptured and the cerebral fluid had come out of my ears, resulting in my remaining conscious through it all, and then healing very quickly. Somehow I had been delivered from the very serious after-effects of the injuries that I had sustained. Often people remain in a semi comatose state for weeks, even months. Some die, but my God had delivered me.

In spite of my extraordinary deliverance, my personal position was very difficult to say the least. I still needed to heal, and complete healing would take some months. I had given up my job because I was expecting to go to England and only planned on being in South Africa for a few of weeks, consequently I had no income. The car that I had intended to sell to pay for my ticket had been badly damaged in the first accident and needed extensive repairs, and I had been damaged in the second accident, and also needed extensive repairs. But, praise God, I was healing rapidly. The accident ward was full to capacity so the hospital administration asked those who were on the mend, if they had someone to look after them, to make room for other serious cases. Fortunately for me a lovely lady from my church said she would look after me, so I was able to stay with her for a number of weeks while I recovered.

In the next few weeks my car was repaired and sold. Unfortunately the proceeds could not go towards the purchase of my air ticket to England, but had to be used to keep me going in South Africa. Three months after my accident I was back on the road, hitch hiking to Zambia. My father had managed to get me a temporary job in Kitwe, a mining town about forty miles from Ndola, my home town. My move to the United Kingdom had to be put off until I was, once again, financially viable.

CHAPTER FOUR

A message from God

Hitch hiking was a way of life. I loved the freedom of standing beside the road with my few possessions, waiting for a lift. I would meet someone that I had never met before, and more than likely we would have a very long and interesting conversation. On this occasion I got quite good lifts, and one of them had a profound effect upon my life. I was standing at the side of the road, somewhere in the Northern Transvaal, when a man stopped and offered me a lift. He was a very friendly gentleman who immediately engaged me in conversation. He asked me where I was going and I told him I was heading for Ndola, Zambia. He asked me why I was going there and I explained that I had just had a car accident, and that my Father, who lived in Ndola, had managed to get me a temporary job. He then asked me what I was going to do after the job came to an end, and I replied that I wanted to go to England to catch up on my studies so that I could go to university. He continued to question me by asking me what I was going to study at university, and for some reason I answered, "possibly social studies." "Why?" He asked. And I replied, "Because I want to help people." Then, to my astonishment he asked, "Why don't you just go to Bible College?" So I answered, "I am a Christian." Amazingly he seemed to know that, and said again more definitely, "I think you should go to Bible College." I then asked him who he was, and he said that he was a travelling Christian book seller, and that's all I ever found out about him.

Sometime later he dropped me off at the side of the road, and I have never seen him again. My suggestion that I might get involved in social studies indicated that I was still wavering in my conviction about studying for the ministry, but this meeting changed everything. I was quite sure that this man was a messenger from God and that our meeting was divine intervention. This was the second time that God had sent someone to tell me to go to Bible College, and humanly speaking this messenger knew nothing about me; he was just obeying God. The first time God spoke to me I was only 19, the second time I was 21, and in between these two incidents there had been a rather inconvenient car accident.

One could ask why God allowed me to go through that very painful experience. I was, after all, trying to get to England to further my studies. I can only conclude that He took me through it all so that I would understand more fully the frailty of my existence. Life can be taken from us in "the twinkling of an eye," therefore we must not take it for granted, but rather should treat it as a gift from God. He gives us life, and He gives us purpose, and I knew that His purpose for me was to preach the Gospel of Jesus. My mind was made up. I was going to Bible College!

About six months later I moved to London where I found lodgings at a place called the Foreign Missions Club, now known as the Highbury Centre. In those days it catered for returning missionaries and Christian workers, and a variety of foreign students, most of whom were studying English and preparing for Christian ministry. I met some extraordinary people while I was there. They were so motivated to accomplish God's will and purpose, and I wanted to be like them.

I worked to support myself and studied to upgrade my school qualifications at the same time so that I could get university entrance. Shortly before the end of my stay I visited

London Bible College, now known as London School of Theology, to have an exploratory interview. The interview must have gone well because I was offered a place at the college, to be taken up at my earliest convenience. My mission accomplished, I returned to South Africa where I planned to work for a year or two to raise the money required for college fees and my own support. However, this took a little longer than expected because I met Muriel, my wife to be, and we were married on the 26th August 1972. Just ten days later we moved to England where, finally, I was able to commence my theological education.

I was not a great student, but the theological training I received was a good foundation for the ministry that has followed. I have now been in ministry for 40 years, and in that time God has done some truly extraordinary things. Some periods of our Christian ministry were not remarkable, and there were difficult times, but praise God there have also been times when God has worked with astonishing power. On some occasions we could explain what had happened scientifically, but we still new it was an act of God. On other occasions there was no scientific explanation for what God had done. This book recalls both the explicable and the inexplicable.

CHAPTER FIVE

Hearing and doing what God says

It would have been easy to stay in England after I had completed my studies – after all I was British by birth, I had a British passport, and I had grown up in a British colony. At the time of my graduation I had only lived in South Africa, on and off, for about five years. South Africa was a difficult country to work in – a pariah in a large part of the world because of its apartheid policy – but what a challenge to be able to do something of real significance in a country with so many obvious problems. Then of course my wife, Muriel, is a South African, and at the time her entire family were still living in the country. But the real reason why we went back to South Africa was that we knew that God wanted us to be there.

It would be easy to tell the story church by church, but it would also be rather laborious. I think it would be much more profitable to look at some of the highlights – those times when we knew God was working in power. It is my experience that God works most powerfully when we are relying on Him completely, when we do not have a plan B, and we know that if God does not come through with the solution we are in real trouble. I started this book by recalling an incident which occurred while I was the pastor of a small church that I had planted on the outskirts of Johannesburg. Now I would like to reveal more fully what we experienced in that period of our ministry.

Before moving to Johannesburg to do church planting, I was the co-pastor of a rapidly growing independent church in Cape Town. In spite of the blessing that we were experiencing, it became clear to us that God wanted us to move to Johannesburg to plant a new work. I realised at the time that it would not be an easy undertaking as I would need to go back into secular work to help support my family. We had four children, Christopher who was eight, and triplets, Jennifer, Joanna, and Stephen who were four. God had blessed us with an unusually shaped family. As you can imagine, they required a lot of attention and care. We arrived in Johannesburg in the middle of a financial downturn and jobs were quite scarce. Fortunately we were able to stay with Muriel's parents at the outset, but that was only a temporary arrangement.

My first priority was to get a job, but that was more difficult than I had expected. I eventually found an advert for a consultant at an employment agency. For some reason, even though I had no experience, I thought that it sounded like my kind of job. It was all about people, and I liked people. I put in my application and got an interview with the owner of the business. At the end of our chat, he told me that he really liked me but that he could not take me on because I had no experience and had not worked in secular work for fourteen years. By this stage I was getting desperate because I needed to support my family and there were not many jobs available. So when I came across an advert for a company representative where the employee had to take all the risk, I took the job. I was required to use my car and my petrol, and they only paid commission on sales with no basic salary.

On the day of commencement I was doing my morning Bible reading. The passage for the day was from Numbers 14:42:

> "Do not go up, because the Lord is not with you.
> You will be defeated by your enemies." (NIV)

I knew God was speaking to me but I was desperate, so I went up anyway. It took me just a day and a half to realise that I should have listened to the Lord. The job was a real dead end, with very little prospect of success. So I stopped working at the hopeless job and decided to go back to my first preference, the employment agency. The following day I went to see if I could get another interview with the owner. I sat in the waiting room for a few minutes and caught him as he was walking through. Fortunately he remembered me, so I asked if he would give me just five minutes of his time. He agreed, and we went into his office for another chat. My approach was to accept my inexperience and to recognize that he was taking a risk if he employed me. Initially he had been offering a large basic salary with a 5% commission on each placement made, so I suggested that he give me a small salary with a 15% commission on each placement I made. "That way" I said, "I am taking the risk." He looked at me with a half smile on his face and said, "With your kind of attitude you may do well at this job. Alright I will take you on."

On the morning that I was due to start, I felt the Lord say to me, "What would you do if I told you not to go up again?" So rather apprehensively I picked up my daily readings book and read the reading for the day which was from Numbers 13:30:

> "We should go up and take possession of the land, for we can certainly do it." (NIV)

I knew the Lord was giving me the go-ahead, so I started my new job with confidence in Him, knowing that He would enable me to do well even though I had no experience. Amazingly, the first month I was there I was the top consultant, because God blesses us when we follow His direction. Once again I have to ask that question, what chance was there of me receiving those two pertinent readings on those two vital days? Surely this was not a coincidence, this was God!

After a period of time we found our own house and we started our new church, but the financial downturn was biting.

My boss had put all the consultants off except for me, and I could see that there was a good chance that I would have to go as well. However, through the consultancy I was able to find myself a good job as a company representative, with a company car, company petrol, and a basic salary and commission which provided for our needs until we needed it no longer.

Our next challenge was to find an appropriate meeting place for our little church. We started by meeting in a restaurant on Sunday mornings when the restaurant was not open for normal business. The surrounds were quite pleasant, but the rent was much too high. I tried to find a public hall or function room, but every hall and room seemed to be occupied, too expensive, or had a waiting list. I was not having much success. The Lord drew my attention to the Apostle Paul's exhortation in Ephesians 6:12:

> "For our struggle is not against flesh and blood, but against the rulers, against the authorities, against the powers of this dark world and against the spiritual forces of evil in heavenly realms." (NIV)

In short, when we are experiencing difficulty in getting God's work done, it is not the people who are the problem – it is the evil one who is deliberately trying to hinder the ongoing work of God. Realising this, I decided to fast and pray. Fasting is encouraged in the Bible to strengthen our praying in difficult circumstances, our Lord Himself encouraged this practice in Matthew chapter 6. We fast when we give up certain pleasures of life, such as eating, to show the Lord that we are serious about our prayer requests. This does not mean, however, that God will always respond positively to fasting. Our requests still need to be within His will and purpose, and when they are He will respond positively, breaking down the strongholds of the evil one in the process.

My circumstances, of course, were a little unusual. As a company representative I would drive around Johannesburg during the day visiting various businesses, so fasting was quite a challenge. On this occasion I decided to leave out breakfast and lunch, and I prayed out loud as I drove around the city. Sometime after two o clock I drove into a parking lot, parked my car, and went in to see a customer. On the way back to my car I felt in my pockets for my keys and realised that I did not have them with me. As expected, the car was locked and the keys were inside the car hanging from the ignition. In those days it was an easy mistake to make as locking was usually done manually, without the keys in hand. Fortunately I knew how to break into my car, but I needed a piece of strong wire. Quite spontaneously I spoke out loud to the Lord saying, "Lord, I need a wire coat hanger." At which point I turned around and to my surprise I saw a wire coat hanger hanging from a fence pole right behind me. In a few moments I had fashioned the wire into the necessary tool and opened the locked door of the car. A short time later I was driving down the road thinking, "wow the Lord is with me, this fasting really works."

We had recently moved into the area and quite near our new home there was a small library. Some libraries had a function room or a small hall attached. I had been watching this particular one on Sunday mornings, and each Sunday smartly clad people were coming and going from the premises, so I assumed there was already a church in residence. But God was with me, so I drove towards the library and parked my car. On the way into the building I noticed a small hall which appeared to be quite adequate for our needs. I approached the receptionist and asked if the hall was for hire, and she said that it was. I asked her if it was available on Sundays, and she replied affirmatively. I then said that I had seen people coming and going on Sundays, and asked if the hall was being used by a church. Her reply was that some churches used it occasionally, but no church had it on a regular basis. Naturally I was excited to say the least, and went on to ask if our church could have it on a regular basis. After a few enquiries about who we were and what we were doing she said that we could. Then, to conclude, I asked her how much the rent was. When she told me that it would be R10.00 a month I was quite taken aback – it was so cheap. So I filled in the form and paid my R10.00 in advance. On my way out she shouted after me, "just a moment, in the small print it says churches don't have to pay at all." She then gave me back my R10.00 and I went on my way rejoicing.

To summarise, I fasted and prayed, and God responded by supplying a wire coat hanger from nowhere so that I could get into my locked car without the key. Then He gave me a free hall for the church to meet in, after months of trying to find a well priced venue without success. So my question once again has to be, how did that happen if God is just a delusion?

The church progressed and we soon grew out of our tiny hall at the library, but God miraculously supplied a custom built church building on the outskirts of the suburb. It was an old farm church built on an agricultural holding with a lot of land. It was just one hall with the essential facilities, such as toilets and an area to make tea and coffee and wash the dishes afterwards and not much else, but we loved it. Our church very quickly became multiracial, and we had our services in English plus an interpretation into one other language. Around the time that we moved there, the resistance to apartheid in the nation was increasing. The schools in Soweto, the huge black township on the outskirts of Johannesburg, were being boycotted by the students protesting against the apartheid policy. As a result, black children with nothing to do started playing football on the church property. Some of the ladies working in our church asked them why they were not in school, and they explained that it was not safe to go to a government school because of the boycott. So these ladies got together and arranged some basic school classes teaching reading, writing and arithmetic.

This was very informal and a little haphazard, but I liked the idea. The children were often related to women who were working as domestic workers for the white families in the local suburb, and after a little while these mothers started attending our church with their children.

I soon realised however, that the teaching we were giving was very inadequate, and what we really needed was a proper school. So with no teachers, equipment, or money to finance the same, I suggested to the church that we start a real school. I assured them that I had some ideas that I thought would work. Actually I had a person in mind who I thought would be the right person to get the school off the ground. She lived in Cape Town and attended my previous church. She was from a missionary family, like myself, and was qualified both as a teacher and a social worker. I was sure that she would be an ideal person to get the school going. I decided to give her a call and was not surprised when she greeted the proposal quite positively. I told her that we could not pay her and that she would have to raise her own support, and she said she would pray about it and let me know when she had an answer from the Lord. A short time later, she phoned me and said that she would be very happy to move to Johannesburg to start the new School.

The school was an immediate success. The children had nothing to do and were quite keen on getting an education. Our teachers were not qualified, but our new head teacher gave them basic training in the required subjects and, in the circumstances, our new school staff did a wonderful job. A charity financed the building of two prefabricated classes, and certain mission organizations became interested in what we were doing so they volunteered their help. But as things gathered pace I realized that I was not coping with my multifaceted job description. I had a full time secular job working normal office hours. In addition to that I was running a church and overseeing the management of the school. This meant I had to raise funds to pay the school staff and collect donated food from factories to feed the children at lunch time.

Raising the funds was my favourite activity. This involved visiting multinational businesses, embassies, and other interested organizations to appeal for funds on behalf of Kingsway School. I loved doing it and I was able to raise a considerable amount of money. However, I soon realised that I was doing too much, and as a result I was neglecting the church. I asked the Lord what I should do about my dilemma, and I felt God say that I needed to give up my secular job – my only source of income – and secondly, that I should stop collecting food for the children. I had no doubt at the time that both of these decisions could make life very difficult. Without my salary we would have to live on Muriel's salary, which was not enough for our family of six. Muriel has faithfully worked for most of our married life, and has been a real blessing from the Lord. I do not know what I would have done without her. But in addition to our family needs, there were also the needs of the children at the school. How would we feed them if I did not collect food from the factories? Fortunately, our God is an awesome God!

Within a week of telling Joan that I could not collect food for the children anymore, a group of four local churches approached us and said that they would like to feed the children. By the second week another church had joined them, so there were five churches that were willing to provide lunch for the children from Monday through to Friday. Now that would have been wonderful if we had put the word out and the churches had responded positively. But actually we told nobody about our dilemma. The need arose, and God supplied the need at exactly the right time. The first four churches just happened to make the offer at the point of our crisis. Our God is amazing! He also looked after our financial needs as a family, sometimes in ways that we could explain, and other times in ways that have no scientific explanation.

CHAPTER SIX

Can we explain everything God does scientifically?

On one occasion, I needed to travel by car to visit someone but realised that I had hardly any petrol left and very little money. Muriel was at work, so I drove to her office, parked the car and went inside to see if she could help. Between us we had R4.78, not much even in those days, but enough to buy a little petrol. The petrol stations in South Africa are labour intensive, so there is always an attendant to help you fill up with fuel and attend to any other service required. Once I had arrived at the petrol station I stopped the car, wound down the window, and told the attendant that I needed petrol to the value of R4.78. I then gave him the key to the petrol cap. After he had put the petrol in the tank he brought back my key and asked me if I would like him to wash the windscreen. I apologized and said that I would not be able to tip him, which was expected, but he said he would do it anyway. While he was washing the windscreen I put the key in the ignition to see how much petrol I had got for my money. To my amazement the indicator went up to about two thirds of a tank, and it had been just about empty. Naturally I was alarmed as I was expecting far less. So I put my head out of the window and asked how much he had put in the tank, emphasizing once again that I only had R4.78. But he assured me that he had only given me petrol to the value of R4.78. There was the possibility, of course, that my petrol tank indicator was malfunctioning, so I took a careful note of the mileage and decided that I would test and see how much petrol I had received. This I did and had to eventually conclude that I had received about three times more than I should have received.

The question is how did that happen? I don't know, somehow God had multiplied the amount of petrol I was meant to receive, and I can't explain how it happened scientifically. Some weeks later I attended a community committee meeting of local residents who had become interested in what we were doing. One of them happened to work for a very large mining company, and at the meeting he told me that the company wanted to give me a car to use for the work we were doing, all expenses included. I thanked him very much and concluded that in addition to miracles that have no scientific explanation, God also uses circumstances which can be explained, but the miracle is in His perfect timing.

This was not the first time that we had experienced God moving in ways that have no scientific explanation. One Sunday evening, in our previous church in Cape Town, I was preaching to a packed congregation, and my sermon was on Jesus' statement about John the Baptist in Matthew 11:11 & 12:

> "I tell you the truth: Among those born of women there has not risen anyone greater than John the Baptist; yet he who is least in the kingdom of heaven is greater than he. From the days of John the Baptist until now, the kingdom of heaven has been forcefully advancing, and forceful men lay hold of it." (NIV)

Quite simply Jesus was saying that until His coming, those who followed God had been limited in what they could do, and with these limitations John the Baptist had accomplished more than anyone else. But as a result of Jesus' coming, God was going to do something far more powerful amongst those who believed in Him. And even the least in God's Kingdom would do greater exploits than John the Baptist had done. However, Jesus made it quite clear that this potential was only available to those who forcefully "lay hold of it," those who make themselves available and step out in faith in very difficult circumstances.

As I was preparing to preach this sermon, I felt God telling me to use the passage in Mark 5:24 – 34, about the "woman who had been subject to bleeding for twelve years." The incident captured my attention because Mark, the Gospel writer, made it clear that the woman had tried every other option. In Verse 26 he says that:

> "She had suffered a great deal under the care of many doctors and had spent all she had, yet instead of getting better she grew worse." (NIV)

Providentially she heard about Jesus, an itinerate preacher who was moving from place to place preaching the gospel of the Kingdom of God and performing miracles of healing. Some said that if you just touched His clothing you would be healed. But the day that she went to receive her healing, verse 24 says:

> "A large crowd followed and pressed around Him." (NIV)

So it was difficult to get close to Him and touch His clothing. But she was determined to receive God's healing, so she made her way through the crowd and touched His cloak. Mark continues in Verse 29:

> "Immediately her bleeding stopped and she felt in her body that she was freed from her suffering." (NIV)

Mistakenly she thought she had managed to get her healing on the quiet, but Jesus knew that power had been transferred from Him to someone else and therefore asked who had touched Him. Eventually the woman confessed, and after telling Jesus her story she received further ministry from the Lord in Verse 34 who said:

> "Daughter, your faith has healed you. Go in peace and
> be freed from your suffering." (NIV)

It occurred to me that this woman had forcefully laid hold of that which God had for her in Christ Jesus. She had pressed her way through the crowd to take hold of her healing. So I used this story as a climax to my sermon and called on all those present who wanted to receive from God what He had for them in Christ Jesus, to come forward. A small crowd responded, but too many came for me to deal with individually, so other members of the congregation helped me pray for them. A few days later, I received a letter from a woman who had been visiting our church on the night in question. She told me that she had the same problem as the woman in the Bible. She, too, had tried everything that conventional medicine could offer but had not been healed. However, on the Sunday evening in question, God spoke to her, urging her to attend our church for the first time so that she could be healed. Someone prayed for her, and she was completely healed.

The question is, was it just a coincidence that I happened to be speaking about the woman who was "subject to bleeding" on the very night that God told another woman, who was "subject to bleeding", to attend our church? Furthermore, can anyone explain scientifically how this problem, which could not be solved by conventional medicine, somehow went away when people in the local church prayed for her healing in Jesus name? I find it very interesting that Jesus, speaking to the woman in the Bible, made it quite clear that it was her faith that had healed her. The same of course could be said about the woman who visited our church, for she too had responded to God in faith, and God healed her.

Healing in Jesus' name is a powerful demonstration of God's existence, both to the one healed, and to those who witness the healing. As we have already seen in Hebrews 11:6 (NIV), the Bible challenges us to trust God to do what He says He can do. That is what the writer to the Hebrews means when he says that God "rewards those who earnestly seek Him." Amazing healings, supernatural provision, and extraordinary guidance become part of our Christian experience.

CHAPTER SEVEN

The spontaneity of the Holy Spirit

Probably the biggest limiting factor in our Christian experience, excluding sin, is our failure to understand the spontaneity of the Holy Spirit. Those who follow Jesus need to be willing to change direction immediately if God so commands, because the Holy Spirit, who guides and empowers the individual believer and the church, is spontaneous in His guidance. God is full of surprises if we are open to the promptings of His Holy Spirit. He does not always tell us to do that which appears to be obvious. Sometimes His choices can even appear quite bizarre. Take Philip for example, chosen as one of the first deacons in the early church, but then was powerfully used by God as an evangelist. Only the Apostles Peter and Paul had a greater impact, when preaching, than Philip had when he addressed the people in Samaria. God obviously had His hand upon Philip. Luke says in Acts 8:6-8:

> "When the crowds heard Philip and saw the miraculous signs he did, they all paid close attention to what he said. With shrieks, evil spirits came out of many, and many paralytics and cripples were healed. So there was great joy in the city." (NIV)

In our day, Philip would have had at least two options open to him if he were to continue in ministry. Either he could have become the leader of the first Church in Samaria, or he could have started a travelling ministry, moving from one town to another, planting churches, then staying awhile to appoint leaders, rather like the Apostles. Maybe he would have done quite well at both of these options, but would either have been God's best?

God obviously wanted to make sure that Philip listened to His next word of direction because He sent an angel, which literally means a messenger, to tell him to do something which most of us would have considered illogical. Luke says in Acts 8:26 & 27:

"Now an angel of the Lord said to Philip, 'Go south to the road – the desert road – that goes down from Jerusalem to Gaza.' So he started out," (NIV)

Philip could have asked "why now, when we are experiencing such blessing in this city?" But because he was in tune with the Holy Spirit, he obeyed immediately. No wonder God blessed his ministry – he was receptive and obedient. In fact, all those whom God blessed in the Bible were those who heard Him and obediently responded to His word. The writer to the Hebrews says in 11:8:

"By faith Abraham, when called to go to a place he would later receive as his inheritance, obeyed and went, even though he did not know where he was going." (NIV)

Likewise, God blessed Philip because of his willing obedience. Shortly after his arrival at the road "that goes down from Jerusalem to Gaza," Acts 8:26 (NIV), a long caravan of vehicles and camels started passing him. In the main chariot there was a very imposing looking Ethiopian eunuch, and to Philip's amazement this Gentile was reading out loud from the Jewish scriptures. In fact, he was reading from Isaiah 53 where the prophet predicts the coming of God's Messiah who dies for the sins of all mankind. Philip, who by this stage must have been walking next to the Ethiopian's chariot, was astonished, and asked him if he understood what he was reading. The Ethiopian, who really wanted to know the meaning, responded by saying in Acts 8:31:

"'How can I... unless someone explains it to me?' So he invited Philip to come up and sit with him." (NIV)

What an amazing opportunity Philip had to share the gospel of Jesus. In his presentation, he must have included baptism as a public declaration of faith because Luke says in Acts 8:36-40:

"As they travelled along the road they came to some water and the eunuch said, 'look, here is water. Why shouldn't I be baptized?' Philip said, 'If you believe with all your heart you may.' The eunuch answered, 'I believe that Jesus Christ is the Son of God.' And he gave orders to stop the chariot. Then both Philip and the eunuch went down into the water and Philip baptized him. When they came up out of the water, the Spirit of the Lord suddenly took Philip away, and the eunuch did not see him again, but went on his way rejoicing. Philip, however, appeared at Azotus and travelled about, preaching the gospel in all the towns until he reached Caesarea." (NIV)

We can't be absolutely sure what Luke meant when he said that "the Spirit of the Lord suddenly took Philip away", but of this we can be sure, Philip listened to the Lord's directions and instructions and followed them in detail. Sometimes God spoke to him through a messenger, and sometimes Philip was moved by God's Holy Spirit within him to do the will of God. In whatever form the instruction came, Philip was obedient and God blessed him. As far as we know, Philip did not return to Samaria where he had made such an impact. When people spoke about the very successful church in Samaria, he resisted the temptation to say, "I started that," because he knew God had started it. Whatever happens in the church, just remember that it is God's work not ours. Secondly, Philip could not have known that the conversion of the Ethiopian eunuch would have such a lasting influence on that nation, and that the church established there would last right up until the present day.

Philip's experience was not unique, for in the book of Acts the followers of Jesus were constantly being led in this way. In chapter 9 Ananias was told in a vision to go and minister to Saul, who became the great Apostle Paul. In chapter 10 God told Peter, through a bizarre vision, to go and share the gospel with Cornelius the Roman centurion. In chapter 13 God's Holy Spirit made it plain to the church at Antioch that Paul and Barnabas should be set apart as missionaries to the Gentile world. In chapter 16 Paul and Silas were actually stopped by God from entering a certain area. Luke says in Acts 16:7:

"When they came to the border of Mysia, they tried to enter Bithynia, but the Spirit of Jesus would not allow them to." (NIV)

Nothing has changed for the believer in the 21st century. God's Holy Spirit still directs those who follow the Lord Jesus in our day. I have certainly experienced God saying both "go" and "don't go." As we have already discovered, God often directs us because He is trying to help someone else. Philip had no idea why God told him to go to the desert road, or that His purpose was to save the Ethiopian eunuch. We, too, should obey God when He gives us His direction – even if we do not understand His purpose. It is wonderful to discover after the event that God has used me in His intricate plan to bless someone else.

CHAPTER EIGHT

God's plans for you and me are perfect

After working in Johannesburg for a number of years, I was called to be the minister of a church in the suburbs of Durban, a large city on the east coast. A great deal of my time was spent in the area which was local to the church, but every now and again I needed to travel, by car, to the city centre to do business. On one of these trips my planned destination was the tax department, which was right in the centre of the city. Upon my arrival, I started to walk along the pavement towards my destination. I crossed over a road from one pavement to another, but when I reached the other side I decided I was going the wrong way, so I turned around and went back across the road to where I had started. At that point, I decided that I had been going the correct way in the first place, so I turned around again and went back across the road. Having reached the other side I started walking down the pavement and nearly walked into a man who I immediately recognized. "Graham," I said, "I haven't seen you for years, what are you doing in Durban?" "Andrew," he replied, "I had heard that you were in Durban, and I was praying this morning that the Lord would help me find you."

Graham had been a member of my Church in Cape Town, but at the time of our meeting we probably had not seen each other for about six or seven years. He had recently lost his job and had travelled to Durban to look for new employment. Unfortunately, that morning he had run out of money. He had paid his hotel bill and had asked the desk clerk to look after his luggage while he went out for several hours. He knew that

I lived in Durban but did not have my contact details, and in a city of two and a half million, that was a problem. So he did what all followers of Jesus should do; he prayed, and God answered his prayer. Humanly speaking, I nearly messed it up by being a little early for God's appointment, so the Lord had me go through my moment of indecision on the pavement, and then brought us face to face with each other. Now if you are not a Christian you could put that all down to chance. But the facts are, Graham asked God to help him find me, and God organized our paths to cross in this rather comical way, on the pavement, in the centre of Durban, which leads me to conclude that God's timing is perfect!

That day, I took Graham home to stay with us so that he would have time to find a job in Durban. I realised at the time that this was a temporary arrangement as we did not really have enough room for him in our home. However, upon enquiry, I discovered and elderly couple who were very happy for Graham to live with them, so he moved in. They looked after him for fifteen months and he became part of their family. It took him a long time to find work, even though he was well qualified, because the country was in the middle of a financial downturn. Graham soon became part of our Church and eventually married one of our ladies. The direction of his life changed completely because God brought us together in response to Graham's prayer for help.

Now it's quite possible that you are thinking that this kind of thing is a once in a life time experience, and I too find it difficult to comprehend how God can be involved in the lives of multitudes of people, all at the same time, and still get His timing absolutely perfect. But let me assure you, He does! In my life I have been on the receiving end of God's perfect timing again and again! Let me tell you just one more short story.

My first Church was in East London, South Africa. Some friends of ours from another church had been witnessing to a friend who had felt a need for God. He wanted to become a Christian, but found it difficult to accept that Jesus is God the Son. So they asked if I would have a chat to him, and I agreed. He came to see me at my house, and we talked about the Lord for some time. At the conclusion of our conversation he still had strong reservations about the person of Jesus, so I closed with a word of prayer and asked our Lord God to give him a revelation of Jesus' true identity. When he got up to go, I led him through the front door of the house to say farewell. Just at that moment a minivan with a huge slogan across the side panel, declaring "Jesus is Lord," drove past the house. My guest was quite overcome when he realized that God had immediately answered my prayer. There was His answer, "Jesus is Lord." What amazing timing, and what a mighty God we serve!

CHAPTER NINE

God encourages personal obedience

It is my experience that God often breaks in supernaturally to get our attention when we are seeking His direction. Because this happens quite often, I sometimes try and set the scene for Him to do just that, only to find that He already has a plan, and His plan is a lot better than mine.

One of the physical consequences of my car accident, all those years ago, is that I have rather weak ears. This became more evident when we moved from Johannesburg, which is six thousand feet above sea level, down to Durban, which is at sea level. Every few months my right ear would firstly get blocked and then, after a week or two, become infected. This was most frustrating when I was conducting a church service, and I had to operate in mono instead of stereo. I found it hard to function in front of a congregation and hard to hear people when I was having a conversation in a large crowd. As a pastor, both of these things happened on a regular basis.

One Sunday morning I woke up and discovered that my ear was blocked again. As I went over my sermon for the first meeting of the morning, I realized that my sermon material was hugely controversial, and I was not entirely sure that I should deliver it exactly as I had prepared it. Perhaps, I thought, I should soften the blow a little. So I made a pact with the Lord. I told Him that I would preach the sermon as it was, if He opened my ear before I arrived at the Church. We lived about two miles from the Church building and driving to the Church was mostly downhill because we were travelling towards the coast. On this particular morning, my ear remained blocked until we were about two hundred yards from our destination, then it opened. But as soon as it opened, I began to rationalize what had happened. On the one hand I had made a pact with the Lord, but on the other hand, sometimes my ear did open anyway as I was going downhill towards sea level. What if this was just a chance event and it had nothing to do with the Lord?

Still wandering what to do, I went into the prayer meeting which preceded our morning service. At a certain point in the prayer meeting a very spiritual lady who sometimes gave me words from the Lord, stopped the person praying in mid – sentence and said "I have a word from the Lord for the pastor." Then speaking directly to me she said, "Pastor, the Lord says you are to preach the sermon that He gave you to preach." That was it! No mistaking the message. The question is how did she know that I had been labouring over that particular issue that morning? Well, she did not know. She was just obediently passing on the message that God had given her.

Now I know that there are those who will take issue with such a claim. The religious leaders of the Jews took issue with the blind man in John 9, who said that it was Jesus who healed him and gave him back his sight. The healing had been done on the Sabbath, and the Jews were not allowed to work on the Sabbath, and as far as the leaders of the Jews were concerned, what Jesus had done was work. Addressing the man they said in John 9:24-25:

> "'Give glory to God... we know this man is a sinner.'
> He replied, 'Whether He is a sinner or not, I don't know. One thing I do know: I was blind but now I see!'" (NIV)

Sometimes I feel a bit like that blind man. People will listen to me as I speak about my experience with the Lord, and then they will try to convince me that God does not intervene in the lives of individuals supernaturally, that it is all pure chance or coincidence. But I am compelled to respond with the same conviction that the blind man had, "I don't care what you say, once I was blind but now I see." We just need to believe that God is able to do the miraculous in our lives.

As a pastor I have spent a lot of time thinking about church growth, both spiritual and numerical, but I have never come to the place where I could say that we have finished the job and that we are now fully grown. The fact is, only God can finish the job. Jesus said in Matthew 16:18:

> "I will build my church, and the gates of Hades will not overcome it." (NIV)

My job as a pastor is to find out what God is doing and to make sure that I fit into His plan. Sometime after I became the pastor of our first Durban church, I was thinking about our future numerical growth. The congregation was growing quite nicely, but we did not have that much space in the main hall. Our property was roughly triangular in shape, bordered by two roads on two sides and a park at the top. But within the triangle at the top left hand side was a private house on private land owned by an elderly couple. The leaders of the church had felt for some time that the only way we could get a larger main hall was to buy the elderly couple's property, knock down the house, and build a new hall. The problem was the previous pastor had tried to persuade them to sell the property and had failed.

As I contemplated what had happened in the past, I wondered whether God had a completely different plan. Instead of growing our congregation into a bigger community, maybe He wanted us to start other congregations in nearby suburbs. So I told the Lord that I would give the idea of purchasing the elderly couples property one more go, and if I was not successful I would have to conclude that His plan was to plant more congregations in the surrounding suburbs. Surprisingly, when I approached them, the couple agreed to sell, but their price was way above market value. They knew that they were in a strong position, and they were going to capitalize on that fact. But I knew that it was not God's plan to buy their property at an inflated price, and I left their home determined to investigate the other option of multiplying congregations.

Some time before this incident I had noticed a piece of property in the suburb next door with a small hall and a larger building, which had been a workshop, standing side by side. After I had left the elderly couple's home, I felt God prompting me to visit that property again, so I went immediately. About twenty minutes later, I was standing outside the smaller hall looking through the window at what appeared to be a large snooker table. I had only been there for about two or three minutes when I realized that someone was standing next to me. A short friendly man, with ginger hair, asked me if I wanted to use the building, and I said that I did. I then asked him who he was and he said that he was the owner. In answer to his next question about my intended use of the building, I told him about my desire to plant a new church. Now unbeknown to me, he was a lapsed Christian with a bit of a guilt complex. He was also quite a successful real estate agent, so when I said I wanted to use the property to start a church, he was quite open to the idea. I asked him how much it would cost to rent the entire property, including the small and the large building. To my surprise, he said I could have the property rent free if I repaired the floor of the large building. We agreed to talk again and I went on my way amazed at what had just happened.

Sometime later we started an evening service in the small hall. To do this, I took the evening congregation from our existent Church and put them in the new building, and this congregation became the foundation of the new work. God put His seal of approval on this new venture as people began to join us from the local community.

Shortly after the launch of the new work, I was walking around the local football field praying, asking the Lord to show me what He wanted me to do in our new locality to bless the community. I felt God saying that we were to declare a great feast, like the wedding banquet that Jesus spoke about in Matthew 22, when He instructed His disciples to go out into the streets and invite whoever was willing to come in and eat. However, I also felt convicted that I should only go ahead if I got a word of confirmation from someone else in the church leadership.

That very night, we had a leader's meeting which commenced with a time of prayer. Not long after we had started praying one of our lady deacons brought a word from the Lord. Her word included an exhortation to the church to declare a great feast and an encouragement for the members of the church to go out into the streets and invite people in. As you can imagine, I was very excited. As soon as she had concluded her word, I told the leaders what God had told me. Right then and there the leadership agreed to be obedient to the word of the Lord, and we began to plan our Great Feast. Once again I have to ask the question, was it just chance that God told me to wait for confirmation through one of my leaders, and that very night the confirmation came, word for word? Or was it God? I am convinced that the events that followed are ample evidence of God's plans coming to fruition.

We decided to hold the Great Feast in the larger building, which by this stage had a new floor. We agreed that we would not print adverts or invitations and that everyone would be invited by word of mouth. As you can imagine, the place was packed, and despite the large number in attendance, everyone was fed. In short the Great Feast was a great blessing. The work continued to grow, and I was content that we were now doing what God wanted us to do in the city of Durban, but I soon discovered that God was not finished yet.

A young leader in my Church, by the name of Brett, kept on telling me that God wanted us to start a work in the centre of the city, but the idea did not interest me at all. I felt we had too much work to do in the suburbs without adding the complexity of city centre work. For quite some time he persisted and I resisted. Then one Sunday morning, at our main congregation, we were having a sharing time when a lady named Vicky stood up to minister, and in essence, this is what she said:

"Last night I had a dream, and in the dream I had somehow got lost in the centre of the city. At the moment of crisis, a police woman came up to me and offered me assistance. She asked if I knew the centre of the city and I said that I did not, so she offered to show me round. She took me to the back streets where there was prostitution and drug dealing, and she showed me inside the apartment blocks where the lifts no longer worked, because no one paid their service charges. She warned me not to be out in the streets on my own because of the muggers. She showed me the vice, the need, and the deprivation, and I heard the Lord say in the words of Isaiah 6:8 (NIV) 'Whom shall I send? And who will go for us?' I woke up crying and said to the Lord, 'Here I am Lord, send me.'"

As Vicky spoke that morning, it was like a knife being thrust into me. Nobody knew my anguish, as far as I knew Brett had only spoken to me about the need of the city centre. After the service I asked Vicky when she had last visited that part of Durban, and she said that, as far as she knew, she had not been there for about fifteen years. I knew God was speaking to me, so I began right away to investigate the possibilities of a new work.

It was around this time that my Father had officially retired. He had served the Lord full time until the age of 78, after which he worked with me, part time, as the pastor for seniors. One day when we were returning together by car from a minister's meeting, I asked Dad if he had the time to go with me to a densely populated area of the city centre. I told him that I had something that I wanted to show him, and he readily agreed to go. A short time later we arrived at the area, to which I felt drawn, and I parked in front of a large block of flats and we got out of the car and stood on the pavement together. "Dad," I said, "I believe God is telling us to start a work in the city centre, but how do I get into this block of flats? How do I start when I don't know anyone here?" Dad had a very simple faith and that's how he managed to accomplish what he did as a missionary in Zambia. He had started a number of churches from nothing. So he put his hand on my shoulder and said, quite simply, "Lets pray." And this is what he prayed. "Dear heavenly Father, you know that Andrew feels called to start a work here in the city centre. If this is your will, we ask that you will open up the way for him, so that he can bring the gospel to this area." Following his prayer, I took him home to his cottage in the suburbs.

Sometime later, I told Muriel that I was going to see if I could make contact with people in that part of the city. She immediately warned me not to go unless I had someone with me. I decided to ask Mike, one of my leaders, if he would be willing to accompany me. He not only agreed, but said he knew a couple who may be interested in our desire to start a new work in the city centre. In fact, the couple he was talking about had attended one of our Alpha courses and were quite keen for us to pay them a visit. The day for the visit arrived, and we went in Mike's car because he knew where they lived and I did not. You can imagine my surprise when we arrived at the same block of flats, in front of which Dad and I had prayed just two weeks earlier, apparently Mike's friends lived on the eleventh floor.

Our visit was an extraordinary success. They were new Christians and they had been fired up by the Alpha course and were praying that God would send someone to start a small group in their home. I know that there are those who would put this all down to chance or coincidence. But isn't God amazing? There are literally hundreds of blocks of flats in the Durban city centre, but God was preparing a couple on the eleventh floor of the block in front of which we had stopped and prayed, just a few days before, that God would give me access, if it was within His will and purpose, and obviously it was!

CHAPTER TEN

God can meet the needs of anyone

We started our new work in the centre of the city with a small group in the flat on the eleventh floor. This group included a wide range of people from different races and backgrounds. One of those who attended was a prostitute who really wanted to follow Jesus. We encouraged her to give up her profession, but she challenged us by asking who would feed her two children if she were to stop prostituting herself. I soon realised that working in the city centre meant that I would have to deal with questions that I had never faced before. But I also discovered that there were answers which I had never thought of before. For example, there was a very nice young lady who used to come for the prayer and Bible study by herself, but when the eats and drinks arrived at the end of the Bible study, she would be joined by her husband, though he never came for the spiritual part.

One day I met this man on the pavement outside. He looked very angry, so I asked him what was wrong. He told me that he worked as a security guard at a brothel and spent most of his time breaking up fights. He shared with me how much he hated what he did. He worked long hours and got paid a pittance, but he could find no other job, so I asked him if he would like me to pray for him. He agreed. Right then and there on the pavement, I put my hand on his shoulder and prayed that our loving heavenly Father would give him a much better job, with a much better salary. The following Wednesday I went to the small group as usual, and to my surprise the man in question was there, with his wife, from the outset. Apparently he had found a new job almost immediately, with a much better salary. He was smiling from ear to ear and wanted to know more about Jesus.

Eventually we had three small groups in the city centre, and someone suggested that we should start a Sunday meeting. I was quite keen but realised that our main problem would be the venue. Ironically there was a church building just around the corner from us which was operating as a stationary shop. Upon investigation, I discovered that it had been closed because the leaders of the church considered the area to be lacking in the kind of population that was open to the gospel. Actually, what they really meant, but could not express, was that the people living in the area were not the kind of people that they were trying to gather. The sad result was the building was lost to those who were willing to preach the Gospel to whoever the Lord would send.

We soon took over a defunct casino and started a Sunday meeting which lasted for about seven weeks, and the people were coming in quite good numbers. Sadly, after this short period, we were told that the owners were going to sell the building and that we would have to move out. I immediately started a venue search. Unfortunately all the venues in the area were commercial and too expensive for us, as we were relying almost entirely on our original congregation for funding. But just at that point, an interesting thing happened. I began to get the feeling that God was going to give us the Central Baptist Church, which, at that time, was a fully functioning church in the centre of the city, with a pastor. Geographically, they were about a mile away from where we were operating, although there was a massive population between us. Our ethos as a church was very different to theirs. We were much less traditional, and our worship style was much more contemporary. Other than that they were evangelical just as we were.

About the time I was deliberating, my brother arrived from New Zealand for a short holiday. He, too, was a pastor and could see that we needed a public meeting for our new work. It was when he asked me what I was going to do about the situation that I first confessed openly that I felt God was going to give us the Central Baptist Church. I remember him asking me how I knew that was going to happen. I told him that I did not fully understand how it would happen, but I had peace in my heart that it would. Sometime later, the association general secretary sidled up to me at a meeting and said that he would like a word. He then went on to tell me that the pastor of the Central Baptist Church was leaving, and the leadership, which was rather old, was not quite sure what they should do next. He said that he knew I was interested in the city centre, and wondered if I would be willing to have a chat to them about my vision for that area. As you can well imagine, I was very interested.

At the appointed time, I addressed the leadership of the Central Baptist Church. I was, to say the least, very enthusiastic about the extraordinary potential of that part of the city. Following my presentation I received a call from the leadership, asking me if I would be willing to become their new pastor. Having prayed about it, I responded by saying that I would be willing, as long as they were happy to share me with two other congregations. Fortunately, they agreed to my proposal, and a new chapter in my ministry commenced. I can't quite remember how long it took, but there came a time when I realised that the work in the centre of the city would more than occupy my time, so I gave up the pastorate of the other two congregations and concentrated on the city centre.

CHAPTER ELEVEN

People from every tribe and nation

God opened up the way for all kinds of ministry. Those who came to the Church came from many backgrounds. Black, white and Asian South Africans, migrants from the countries to the north, particularly the Congo, Rwanda and Burundi, all joined the Church. It was also the time when those known as returnees were coming back to South Africa following the end of apartheid. Some of them came to our Church with fascinating stories of God working in their lives. One lovely man told me his story.

Many years before, when apartheid had a vice grip on the country, this man was a student at a technical college, where he was learning a trade. The irony was that once he was qualified, he would not have been allowed to practice the trade because he was black. As his year moved towards graduation some of the students approached him, as the leader of the student union, indicating that they intended to protest in the streets. That kind of behaviour was strictly forbidden by the apartheid government, and my friend knew it would be dangerous, so he tried to dissuade his associates from any such action. Unfortunately they would not be put off and went ahead as planned without him. Sadly, even though he did not participate, as the student leader he became a wanted man despite his innocence. The result was that he had to flee the country.

In exile he joined one of the resistance movements and there he trained to fight as an insurgent. But the day before he was due to re enter South Africa, to start his new career as a resistance fighter, he was lying on his bed in his room contemplating his future, when he heard a scratching sound coming from the door. Someone had pushed a piece of paper under the door, which turned out to be an anonymous note, asking the question: "If you die tomorrow, do you know where you are going?" He was stunned, because he realised that he did not know where he was going. He had grown up in the evangelical church, but at the time of the incident he knew that he was not following God. Immediately he decided on a change of direction and the following day he refused to go back to South Africa to fight. At first the organization that he had trained under put him in jail, but eventually allowed him to go free. He managed to get to Kenya where he lived in exile for a number of years and married a delightful Kenyan lady.

Once apartheid was abolished, he returned to South Africa with his wife. Shortly after they had settled in Durban, his home town, he expressed his desire to go back to church. His wife, who was a catholic, took him to the local Catholic Church, but he was not happy there. One Sunday morning he went in search of a church and discovered the Durban Central Baptist Church. The first Sunday he attended Church, he put his faith in Jesus, and became a newborn Christian. "At last", he said. "I know where I would go if I were to die tomorrow." I soon discovered that centre city ministry was absolutely fascinating, but also different, in many ways, to the kind of ministry that we had experienced in the suburbs. One of the reasons for this difference was that people came and went so quickly, which meant that our time of influence was often very short, but if that influence was of God it could still last forever!

CHAPTER TWELVE

The blessings of transient ministry

One Sunday I had just finished the morning service, which included communion, when a young man came up to me and asked if he could talk to me. He introduced himself as a student of the University of Westville, studying for a master's degree. He then went on to tell me his story. As a very young man he had left the country to join one of the resistance movements. He did not tell me how much he had been involved in actual armed resistance, but he said that there were a number of questions about life for which the freedom movement had no answers. It appeared that he had not had much contact with the evangelical church in his youth, and he was fascinated with our communion service. He knew instantly that it emphasized fellowship and community. He understood that Jesus' death and resurrection not only made it possible for people to be saved from sin, and to become the children of God, but that they also became brothers and sisters in the Lord Jesus Christ. Having expressed his need for such an experience, he surrendered His life to the Lord Jesus that day.

He only stayed at our church a few months because his degree course soon finished. About a year later, I was watching the news on national TV when the announcer introduced the new chief executive of a significant organization. To my surprise it was our recent convert. I was further surprised when he introduced himself by saying that he was taking up the position because he was a Christian and wanted to show the compassion of Christ. I have never seen him again, but one thing I know is that we, as a church, had been used by God to introduce him to the Saviour.

About this same time, the church received a large influx of asylum seekers, mostly from Franco Africa. Those who came to us were from the Democratic Republic of Congo, Burundi, and Rwanda. I remember one group of twelve arriving together, all related. There were two men and their wives, an unmarried younger brother, and seven children between them. When they arrived at our church they had been in the city for three weeks. They had been offered food and help by one centre, if they converted to Islam, and this was after they had been deprived of both for some days. However, one of the ladies put it powerfully when she said, "I could not lose my precious Lord Jesus." They had also experienced a lot of persecution from the local people who saw them as opposition in the difficult job market. When they arrived at our church they had been without adequate food, sleep, or shelter and on the move in the streets for about three weeks. I was truly blessed when I saw how our folk welcomed them and cared for them.

Two elderly sisters in our church found them temporary accommodation in their own block of flats. Another unlikely host was a single Afrikaans lady, who worked for the police department. On Sundays she had open house at her one bedroom flat and often fed a dozen or more people. At the time, unbeknown to me, she had a terminal disease. When she died two years later, her family held the funeral in an Afrikaans church, which just a few years before would have excluded black people. On that day the chief mourners were black people weeping for Mama Cootzee.

We decided to set up an office to help asylum seekers find work, and if necessary, get the right training to qualify for the available jobs. Many of those who attended were already well educated, having university degrees and other good qualifications, but because they were asylum seekers, they often ended up as car guards or watchmen. I remember going to see a couple from Burundi, both of whom had master's degrees, and they were living in one room with four children, three little girls and a baby boy. He had asked me to visit them in their home and I was very happy to do so. When I arrived, the shared bathroom opposite their room had water leaking under the door and into the passage; apparently this was not unusual. They had been waiting for my arrival so that I could participate in their family Bible reading. The three little girls, dressed in their Sunday best, stood up and sang the song "Arise and shine and give God the glory." And then the father asked me to read from the Bible. Afterwards he spoke to me alone and said "all I want is some country to accept me and my family, so that we can live an ordinary life." I can't express how their plight affected me. I felt like I personally was carrying the burden

The people in the Church were doing a grand job, but it was not enough, so I went to the Lord to find out what He wanted me to do. Fortunately God showed me quite clearly that I could not meet everyone's need, but He could! What I needed to do was pray! So this I did, gladly handing the burden over to the Lord. I told the people that I did not have the answer to all their needs, but God did, and God began to answer prayers in a profound way.

CHAPTER THIRTEEN

"Ask and it will be given to you"

One Sunday morning, having finished the sermon, I made an appeal for all those who had needs to come forward for prayer. Among the needy was a well dressed white man I had never seen before. To be completely honest, he was not the kind of person I was expecting to respond to the appeal. When I asked him what he wanted me to pray about, he said quite simply that he had a financial problem, no different to most of the others in front of me. So I laid hands on him and prayed that God would meet his need in Jesus' name. The following week I received a letter from him in which he explained how he came to visit our church, and how God had answered his prayer.

Apparently he had a small real estate business selling houses, but things had gone wrong. It had all started when his son had asked him to financially back his new business venture. Sadly, this venture had failed, and the father was liable for his son's debts. The bank interest rates in South Africa were very high at the time, which resulted in him paying back interest only and no capital. However, after I prayed for him on the Sunday, an extraordinary thing happened. He received a letter from the bank which acknowledged that he had already paid an amount in excess of the original debt, but still owed a large sum of money due to the excessive interest rates. They explained that they had decided to be lenient and would therefore consider his debt paid in full. I have never in my entire life heard of a bank doing such a thing. I was so surprised that I kept his letter. When I visited him after the event, he told me that he attended another church, and he had only attended our church on that particular Sunday because of God's prompting.

But how did that happen? Those who believe that God is a delusion would say that this was the result of pure chance and the compassion of a bank manager. Well, let's put aside, for a moment, the rather laughable idea of a compassionate bank manager, and recognize that this white, middle class man attended our very multi-cultural church in the centre of the city, just once, because God told him that if he did, he would get his prayer for help answered positively – and that's exactly what happened. Frankly, I am of the opinion that an atheist needs more faith to believe that this was due to chance, than I do to believe that this was due to the Almighty God!

Another ongoing problem was disappointed job seekers from other parts of South Africa, who were stranded in our city because they had no money to get home. The Church was unable to help them, so I did my best out of my own resources, but I could not keep up with the bottomless pit of need. In obedience to the Lord's direction, I stopped giving out money and just prayed that God would meet their need. On one occasion a man came to me with the usual request. I responded by saying that God would supply his need, and all we needed to do was pray. This I did, then I sent him on his way and encouraged him to trust God. The following day he came back to me, smiling from ear to ear, to thank me for my prayers. He then told me how God had supplied his need. Following my prayer he had gone down to the beach front and sat on a bench, looking out to sea. He was very down and was crying to himself. A lady, nearby, noticed his distress and asked him if there was anything she could do for him. He responded by telling her his story, and to his amazement she took out her purse and gave him the required amount to get his return ticket. He was truly blessed, and the best part was that his faith in God, who can intervene in our lives to overcome adversity, was greatly strengthened, and so was mine!

CHAPTER FOURTEEN

Whose blessing do we seek?

The most dangerous form of false doctrine emanating from the Church is doctrine which is near the truth, but not the truth. The more extreme forms of "prosperity teaching" fall into this category. Although this teaching started in the U.S.A., it has thrived in Africa. Sadly, it is often the ministers who end up living lavishly while their congregations continue to experience need. On one occasion, while having a discussion with my father about this heresy, I pointed out that certain verses in the Bible are taken out of context by those who follow this teaching. The result is vulnerable people are duped into parting with their money, and unscrupulous preachers are enriching themselves at their congregation's expense. A good Old Testament example would be Malachi 3:10:

> "Bring the whole tithe into the storehouse, that there may be food in my house. Test me in this says the Lord Almighty, and see if I will not throw open the floodgates of heaven and pour out so much blessing that you will not have room enough for it." (NIV)

Under Old Testament law the tithe was a tenth of all their income, both in goods and finance, which had to be given to the work of God. In return, God promised to bless them materially as well as spiritually. Sadly, people have abused this teaching so that personal enrichment becomes the motivation for following God. People are encouraged to give more and more, and as a result both the church and the minister's income increase. Undoubtedly this teaching is heresy and needs to be put right. However, it is important to recognize that God does promise to bless those who entrust all they have to Him. To back up what I was saying to my father, I told him what had happened to me some years prior to our conversation, while I was working in Cape Town.

My church wanted me to go to a conference in East London, South Africa, but I did not want to leave my wife Muriel on her own to look after our five year old son and our one year old triplets. An obvious alternative was to take my five year old son with me, because friends in East London were willing to look after him while I attended the conference. The problem was that I did not have the money to pay for his air fare. So I decided to sell an almost new motor scooter, which I no longer used, so that I could buy my son a ticket with the proceeds. Prior to this I had hoped to sell the motor scooter and use the proceeds to buy myself a good tape deck, as mine had broken. But I had kept this desire to myself, and not even my wife knew of my intentions. Sometime later I took the motor scooter to the auction mart and watched someone buy it at the sale. I then took the proceeds and purchased an air ticket for my son. A couple of weeks later, back from a very good conference and a valuable time of bonding with my son, I went to the Sunday evening meeting at our church. As I was walking towards my car after the meeting, one of my close friends came up to me and said, "Andrew, I have got something for you, come with me." He then took me to his car and opened the boot, out of which he took a box and handed it to me, saying, "God told me to give you this." Inside the box there was a really good tape deck. How did that happen? I had told no one what I had thought or done.

Having recalled my experience, I asked my dad the same question that I have been asking all the way through this book. How did that happen? I agreed with him that prosperity teaching was neither biblical nor helpful. But I dared to suggest that God does bless us, even materially sometimes, when we are obedient to His word. Dad, who had along with my mother, served the Lord for many years as a missionary, spent most of his life giving away almost everything he owned. As an evangelical Christian from the old school, he believed that God's people should live frugally – especially those who served as ministers of the Gospel. At the time we agreed to disagree, and I returned home. About three weeks later Dad phoned me, excited as he spoke, and he told me what he had just experienced.

In South Africa, in those days, there was a custom followed by some retired ministers of the church who had not contributed to a pension fund, and consequently had no financial support for retirement. They would put on a dog collar as proof of identity, and carry a stamped, headed document on which contributions could be entered, and then go from door to door asking for financial help. As you can imagine, this was open to huge abuse, so that the genuine, retired ministers, suffered because of those who were not genuine. One day my father responded to a knock at their door, and there was a man collecting for his retirement. Normally the respondent would have given him a few Rand, and then bidden him farewell, but my father invited him in. My mother then cooked him a good breakfast and sat him down at the dining room table where they had a chat. After that Dad gave him a suit, shoes, some money, prayed for him and then sent him on his way rejoicing.

The following day Dad received a telephone call from an unknown gentleman who asked if he was the Reverend George Smith, minister of the local Baptist Church, and my father confirmed that he was that man. The caller then said that he understood that my father was in need of a new suit of clothes. Dad was rather taken aback and did not know how to reply. The man then encouraged him to come to his shop in the centre of the town and gave him the address. Very curious as to what would happen next, my father obediently went to the centre of the city and visited the shop, which turned out to be a gents outfitting shop. The owner, a very pleasant gentleman, then gave him a new suit, a shirt and tie, and a pair of shoes and socks, and sent my father away quite bemused at what had just happened to him. He phoned me immediately to tell me about his experience, and how he now understood what I had been talking about just a few weeks before. Once again we have to ask the question, "How did that happen?" Dad never discovered whether there was any connection at all between the two incidents, but he was quite willing to believe that God had organized the two to coincide.

I have no doubt that there are times when our Father God gives us a loving hug to let us know that He is blessed by our obedience. Jesus, in His teaching, encouraged His followers to be open with the Father about their needs, and He promised that the Father would meet those needs. In Matthew 7:7-11 Jesus says:

> "Ask and it will be given to you; seek and you will find; knock and the door will be opened to you. For everyone who asks receives; he who seeks finds; and to him who knocks the door will be opened. Which of you, if his son asks for bread will give him a stone? Or if he asks for a fish will give him a snake? If you, then, though you are evil, know how to give good gifts to your children, how much more will your Father in heaven give good gifts to those who ask Him?" (NIV)

In Luke's version of the same teaching Jesus seems to be talking about spiritual rather than material needs. He concludes in Luke 11:12-13:

> "If you then, though you are evil, know how to give good gifts to your children, how much more will your Father in heaven give the Holy Spirit to those who ask Him?" (NIV)

In John 15:16, Jesus says to His disciples:

> "You did not choose me, but I chose you and
> appointed you to go and bear fruit – fruit that will last.
> Then the Father will give you whatever you ask in my
> name." (NIV)

This promise, that we will receive whatever we ask for in
Jesus name, comes in the context of our remaining in a very
close relationship with Jesus, and doing the will of God, so
that we can bear spiritual fruit. Our Lord is passionate about
our need and hugely saddened by our greed. Much of the
21st century prosperity teaching revolves around greed, not
need. In 1 John 5:14-15 John says:

> "This is the confidence we have in approaching God:
> that if we ask anything according to His will, He hears
> us. And if we know that He hears us – whatever we ask
> – we know that we have what we asked of him." (NIV)

Whatever I request from God must be in accordance with His
will. The whole purpose of praying is that I may understand
what it is that He wants for my life. If the content of my prayer
is designed to persuade God to give me the things I want, I am
wasting my time and His. When I became a Christian, I
surrendered the leadership of my life to Jesus, He became my
Lord and Saviour, and I acknowledged that He always knows
what is best for me. If my fellowship with Jesus is real He will
not only let me know what His will is, He will give me whatever
I need so that it may be accomplished. I have certainly
experienced that again and again as I have walked together
with my Lord and Saviour. The process of prayer is not just an
individual talking to God. That would be like a one sided
telephone call, with you on the one side, talking away, and
never hearing what the person on the other side is saying.
What use would that be? When I spend time talking to God I
also need to listen to what He has to say to me in reply.

God speaks to us in a number of ways. Sometimes He replies to our prayer requests immediately. For example, you will pray and then stop for a while to reflect, and ideas will flood into your mind, and you will realise that God is giving you those ideas. He is answering your prayer. On another occasion, you will bring your request to God and get no answer at first. The reason is, God's timing is perfect, and we need to wait for Him to answer in His perfect time.

It's also important to recognize that answers to prayer come through different channels. Sometimes God will speak to you personally, and within your spirit you will know that it is God, and you will understand what He is saying. On other occasions God will speak to you through fellow Christians, just like the lady in my congregation in Durban, who stopped the prayer meeting before the service, to tell me that God wanted me to preach the sermon that He had given me; only I knew that I was wrestling with that very issue. Then of course God uses His Word the Bible to give us extraordinary answers to prayer. I am often amazed at the answers I get from God's Word about direction, about people, and about the Christian life in general. Finally, do not forget that God also uses circumstances. I am referring to those occasions when we ask God to help us to know His will, and as we move forward we experience the hand of God opening doors and closing doors, and we are at peace because we know it is God. John speaking in Revelation 3:7-8 says:

> "These are the words of Him who is holy and true, who holds the key of David. What He opens, no one can shut, and what He shuts no one can open. I know your deeds. See, I have placed before you an open door that no one can shut." (NIV)

How wonderful it is to know God moving in this way, and if you walk closely to Him you will experience Him doing it again and again.

CHAPTER FIFTEEN

Moving countries again

A few years after arriving in Durban I was confined to bed with a bad dose of flu. Fortunately I love to read, so I took out the biography of Charles Haddon Spurgeon and began to read about his ministry in central London in the 19th century. I was soon captivated by this man and his extraordinary vision for God's work in that great city. My time in bed went by far more quickly than expected, and the reading of Spurgeon's biography had an unexpected impact on me as an individual. I felt the Lord saying quite clearly that one day He would move me to the centre of London, where I would work for Him. I knew that it would not happen quickly, but it would happen eventually. The fact is we continued to minister in Durban for another seven years before the Lord allowed me to move on.

I was born on the 19th of August 1947, in Sevenoaks, Kent, just south of London, England. My parents lived just up the road in a town called Biggin Hill. The London that I felt drawn to was very different to the one my parents had left 52 years before. No longer were the majority from an Anglo Saxon background, but people from every tribe and nation lived and worked in the city, and the opportunity to preach the gospel was as great as it had ever been.

Some years after reading Spurgeon's biography, I was walking around a cemetery near our house in Durban. The cemetery was on a hill overlooking the city. I loved to go there to pray over the city and to listen to the Lord. On this occasion I felt the Lord say quite clearly that the time to go to

London had arrived. Three of my children were already in England; one at university, one at theological college, and one working in London. My Dad and Mom were in their late eighties and living in a cottage just down the road from us. Dad had been quite ill and had already had one serious operation. Mom and Dad were both British pensioners, so I knew that I could take them with me if they so desired.

I realised that the hardest part would be to leave the church in Durban; it was going exceptionally well, for which we were deeply grateful. God had been so good to us! What if I had heard wrong, and I was meant to stay in South Africa? Moving countries is a big step, but moving continents at the age of fifty four is a huge step, and not something I would do unless I really knew God was in it. But I could not get the thought out of my mind. God was saying quite clearly that the time to go to London had arrived. Muriel was not surprised when I told her what the Lord had said to me, partly because we had talked and prayed about the possibility before, and partly because, through our lives together, Muriel had become accustomed to uprooting and moving on in obedience to the Lord's command.

We decided that I would go first, so that I could investigate the opportunities for ministry in the centre of London. Muriel would remain in South Africa with our daughter Joanna, who unlike her siblings, had not already left for the United Kingdom. The idea was that the two of them would follow once I had got properly settled in London. I should have realised that things are never quite that simple. Ten days before we were due to leave South Africa, my Dad, who was 88, went to be with his Lord and Saviour. It had been difficult winding up my parent's affairs before he died, but after he died, the task was much greater. I had to arrange a funeral for my Dad, look after my Mom who had just lost her husband, and then leave South Africa with her to settle in England.

My Dad's funeral was amazing! Looking back, I don't think he was ever meant to leave Africa, because he loved the African continent and the African people with an extraordinary passion, so God took him directly home from the continent he loved.

When we arrived in England, I took my Mom to stay with my brother Malcolm, who had moved to England a couple of years before me. I then found lodgings in London and began my search for the ministry the Lord had prepared. This is probably a good time to mention that just because I was involved in God's work, things did not fall into place in a miraculous fashion. When we read the New Testament, especially the book of Acts, we get the impression that God was doing a miracle a minute. But in actual fact, life for the average Christian of that time was not easy. The record that we have in the New Testament is the record of extraordinary events over quite a long period of time and represents a large group of people. The New Testament records the highlights and the difficulties that God's people experienced in those early days of the Church. So what I am about to relate to you is a mixture of highlights and difficulties, and I am grateful for both, because if I had never had the problems, I would not have experienced God's glorious deliverance from the same.

Most of my difficulties, at the outset, resulted from a mistaken idea that God was going to use me as an evangelist, not a pastor. Even though I had been a pastor for 25 years, I was tired of overseeing a church, and I rather liked the idea of being an evangelist. I ignored the fact that God had made it quite clear to me that I would be based in the centre of London, and I spent a lot of time trying to find some organization that would employ me as an evangelist. Without going into detail, it would be sufficient to say that I failed miserably. At the same time I had to finance my existence, so I worked spasmodically for a group of immigration solicitors, and in the process managed to survive. My job was to escort asylum seekers to the Home Office in Croydon (London) and Liverpool. It was not the job that I wanted to do, but it was very interesting. I did not realise at the time how much this experience would help me in the years to come when many people from across the globe, with all kinds of immigration needs, would join my church in the centre of London. God can even use our difficult times to benefit His plan and purpose.

Once I realised that I was not going to be an evangelist, I made contact with the Baptist Union of Great Britain and applied to be accredited as a Baptist minister. Up to that time, my accreditation had been limited to southern Africa. I was reliably informed that this process would take a few months. Unfortunately, I had already wasted a lot of time and was keen to get on with the job. Quite early on in the process, the London Baptist Association contacted me and asked if I would go and have a look at a particular church which needed a pastor. The idea was that I would visit them on a Sunday, just to be part of the congregation, but I would not need to preach.

I did not have much to do at the time, so I decided to go and look at the area during the week, before visiting the church, just to get a feel of the place. One thing led to another, and very soon I was I popping my head in the front door of the church and disturbing some ladies who were having a keep fit class. To say the least, they were not happy with my intrusion. I think they thought I was a "peeping tom." On my way back to the station, I walked past a large, well known Baptist Church, which was open to the public. I decided to pop in and look around. A very friendly couple gave me some tea and introduced me to their pastor, who, having established my credentials, asked me if I would like to preach at his church. In the weeks that followed I preached there twice.

How I wished that they were the church that was looking for a pastor.

On the way home I felt the Lord say quite clearly that I was not going to be the pastor of the church to which I had been sent. Unfortunately for me, they were still expecting my visit the following Sunday morning, so I decided to go anyway. I set out early, but when I arrived at the station I discovered that it was closed. Wondering what to do next, I consulted my A to Z, city map book, and calculated that I could walk to the next tube station and catch the train there, and still be on time. As I walked along the road I felt the Lord saying again and again, "You're wasting your time, you're not going to be the pastor of that church." So I decided to go to the next station, and if that too were closed, I would know that God was definitely closing the door. However, when I arrived at the next station it was not closed. I headed upstairs to the appropriate platform, where a man in uniform politely informed me that there would be no trains that day. I never discovered why the trains were cancelled. Perhaps the Lord organized it to make sure I would listen to His word of warning. I did not hear about that church again until just recently, about fourteen year later, when someone informed me that it was a complete disaster, destroying three pastors in a row. I am so grateful that the Lord protected me, and I am here to give God the glory.

Things did not go particularly well for some time after that. I was working spasmodically for the immigration solicitors and living in one room in the home of a very kind Christian lady. I missed my wife, and I got quite despondent. One day while walking on Tooting Common, I cried out to the Lord in anguish, "Why have you brought me to this God forsaken place?" What a question for a preacher of the Gospel to ask. When I got home I picked up a daily readings book, which had been given to me years before by one of my sons.

The reading was from Proverbs 23:18:

> "You have a wonderful future ahead of you.
> There is hope for you yet!" (TLB)

God's timing is perfect. We could explain the whole incident away as mere chance, if it were not followed by God's extraordinary provision. At first I was still angry, but then I asked the Lord for help and forgiveness and told Him once again how much I loved and needed Him. After this things began to happen.

CHAPTER SIXTEEN

Getting back on track

Recognizing that God had told me that my ministry would be in the centre of London, and having a strong impression that God was going to show me a Church, I went on a walkabout in the centre of the city. After about three hours, I walked past The King's Cross Baptist Church. Immediately I was interested. The position was very central and the area was a bit run down, but in my estimation it definitely had promise. I wanted to find out if they had a pastor, so I looked at their signboard and was disappointed to discover a pastor's name in the appropriate place. However, a short time later I received a letter from the London Baptist Association, and with the letter was a list of churches in London looking for a pastor. I read the list with interest and was hugely encouraged when I saw the name of The King's Cross Baptist Church. Apparently their pastor had just left and they had not yet removed his name from the board.

I immediately gave the London Baptist Association a call and spoke to one of the regional ministers, telling her that I was interested in The King's Cross Baptist Church. She responded enthusiastically, letting me know that a meeting was planned for the following week, when they would try to match pastors looking for positions, with churches looking for a pastor. She promised to put my name forward, as a possibility, for the position at the King's Cross Church. Under the Baptist system, that is as far as they can go; they can just make suggestions, but it is the local Church who chooses the pastor. Following our conversation, I waited for some weeks for a reply, but nothing happened, so I phoned the LBA office and spoke to the same person again. She told me that at the meeting they were obliged to recommend someone else before me. Unfortunately my accreditation had not yet come through, so at the time of the meeting I was not yet a Baptist Union minister.

I was disappointed, to say the least, but I was not yet finished, and neither was the Lord. As is often the case, I asked the Lord to give me guidance from my daily reading of His Word. That day the reading was from Acts 4:13-21 where Peter and John were brought before the Sanhedrin and told not to preach any longer in the name of Jesus. But in response Peter and John asked a very important question. Acts 4:19:

> "Judge for yourselves whether it is right in God's sight
> to obey you rather than God." (NIV)

I knew God was talking to me. If He wanted me to be the pastor of The King's Cross Baptist Church, it did not matter what people said, even good people. I must obey God rather than man. By that time Muriel had joined me in London, so I shared my feelings with her. I suggested that we attend the church at King's Cross the following Sunday morning, and she agreed. When we arrived there was a small crowd of about 35 adults, plus teenagers and children. We sat down about four rows from the front on the right hand side, and as we did, I knew I had found the church where God wanted me to serve Him. I remember saying to Muriel, "this is where we are going to be." She put her finger on her lips and indicated that I should not say that out loud, but I said it again – I could not help myself – "this is where we are going to be." I was that certain.

This is probably the only church I have ever attended where I found the notices the most compelling part of the proceedings. At the appointed time, one of the leaders got up to tell us about the programme for the week. I remember one item in those notices vividly, because the man in question told the congregation that there would be a visiting preacher the following Sunday, the 17th of the month. He encouraged them to listen carefully, as the visiting preacher was looking for a permanent position, and could possibly become their minister if they felt so led by God. As he made this announcement, I felt the Lord say to me, "and you will preach on the 24th." We continued with the service, and at its conclusion we were invited to stay for tea or coffee, which, would be served in the entrance hall of the Church.

Over tea I got into conversation with a lady standing next to me. She asked me where I was from, and I replied that I was visiting from South Africa. She then asked me what I did for a living, and I told her I was a pastor. Her third question opened the door, because she asked me why I had visited their church. I responded by saying that God had sent me, and then added my own question, "do you have anything for me to do?" Now I did not know, at the time, that she was the lady who signed up the preachers, and apparently she endeavoured to sign them up for a good many weeks ahead. However, someone had dropped out on the 24th of that month, so without any hesitation she asked me if I could preach on the 24th. I resisted telling her that God had told me during the service that I would preach on the 24th, but I did tell her that I would gratefully accept the invitation.

Two Sundays later, I was privileged to preach my first sermon at the church in King's Cross, and felt in my heart that it had gone well. After the service, the leading deacon came to me and told me that the deacons had met briefly while we were having tea, and wanted to know if I was interested in a call to ministry. If so, I was to meet with them at an agreed time in the future. I replied that I was interested and would be very happy to meet with them, and so began the process of my being called to be the pastor of The King's Cross Baptist Church. But once again I have to ask the question, how did that happen? By now you know what my answer will be, and I hope you will agree that God's timing and planning are perfect. We just need to be walking closely to Him so that we can hear and do what He tells us to do. I am not writing this to indicate that I have got the whole thing worked out perfectly; I don't, but I know that God does, and I need to trust Him completely. As John says in Revelation 3:7:

> "What he opens, no one can shut, and what He shuts no one can open." (NIV)

I have experienced God firmly close doors and wonderfully open doors. I know without a doubt that this was not random chance – this was God!

CHAPTER SEVENTEEN

Working in the centre of London

Apparently, London has more people groups than any other city in the world. It is for this reason, amongst others, that it also has the greatest potential of any city on earth, to reach the world with the Gospel of the Lord Jesus Christ. When I first became the pastor of the King's Cross Church I asked God how I could accomplish His work in the given situation. We had a large old Victorian building in a bad state of repair. We had about thirty five people in attendance, excluding teenagers and children, and although the people were good Christians, and the leaders loved the Lord, they did not really expect God to bless them. Every idea I took to them they dismissed with the same objection; they had tried it before and it did not work. One day I preached a sermon from Philippians 3:12-14 where the Apostle Paul encouraged his readers to do their utmost to lay hold of everything that God had for them in Christ Jesus, and he emphasized the point by using himself as an example in verse 13-14:

> "Forgetting what is behind and straining towards what is ahead, I press on toward the goal to win the prize for which God has called me heavenward in Christ Jesus." (NIV)

I told the congregation that God's Gospel of salvation was for all people everywhere. It did not matter who they were, if God's Holy Spirit was at work, people would turn to the Lord and be saved from their sin. I encouraged them to forget what was behind them, and to "press on toward the goal to win the prize for which God (had) called (them) heavenward in Christ Jesus," adding that I never again wanted to hear the excuse that they had tried this or that, and it did not work. Thankfully they responded positively, and God graciously saved a good number of people in the years that followed.

Soon after arriving I realised that I would not be able to do much of significance on my own. The Baptist system stresses autonomy. We are not part of a denominational system with each church taking direction from the denominational headquarters, and getting financial assistance from the central body. Each Baptist church is autonomous and must look after its own financial and personnel needs. However, the centre of London is very expensive, and running a large building, housing and paying staff, and reaching out to diverse communities, all takes a lot of money which needs to be raised locally. From the outset I realised that I would need to get assistance from sources other than the membership of the church. I felt the Lord prompting me to seek alliances with other mission organizations working in the city. I had no idea how I was going to do this, so the Lord got the process going for me.

It was quite clear from the start that ministry opportunities were manifold, and a uniform approach was not going to work, so I prepared to do targeted evangelism. Prior to my arrival some folk had joined the church because they thought it would be a good centre for helping the needy. When I arrived there was already a small group of people working with the "street community": among whom there are those who are jobless, homeless, directionless, and often, but not always, addicted to drugs or alcohol. Having been involved in the social implications of the gospel in South Africa, I was all for this kind of ministry in London.

I soon discovered, however, that most of those in need in the centre of London are in a totally different category to those in need in the city centres of South Africa. In the latter a large proportion of the needy will respond positively to the solutions offered by the church, because they have been historically disadvantaged by the state system and long to get out of their predicament. However, those in trouble in London have a state system which is geared to help them, but many still fail to overcome their difficulties because of mental breakdown, substance abuse, and other maladies that cause a sense of hopelessness. Praise God, not all of the needy are in these categories, and there are those who overcome their difficulties with the help of the Lord.

About eight months after we arrived at King's Cross, a married couple who were keen to be involved in ministry, joined the church. Prior to their arrival, both of them had worked for the London city mission; when they arrived the wife still did, but her husband, who had suffered with poor health, had been medically boarded. However it soon became obvious that he had the time, the gifting, and the desire to get involved in our ministry, so he started to help with the work amongst the street community. In spite of his ill health he was doing a good job, and when the person running our drop in centre left the church, he took over. His increased involvement seemed to coincide with his improving health, to the point that I started to wonder whether the London City Mission would consider reinstating him as a full time employee, and then second him to our church. With his permission I made an appointment to see the director, who, to my delight, happily agreed to do as I suggested. Not long after that Donald became our first addition to the pastoral staff, and he and his wife Dorina became a huge asset to the work of the King's Cross Baptist Church, much loved by the people.

CHAPTER EIGHTEEN

Good times and difficult times

Like all churches, we had our good times and our difficult times. After three years as the pastor, I realized that some of my more prominent members were not in agreement with my vision for the church and the area. Due to the lack of agreement, we were not really growing spiritually or numerically. I knew that without the unity of the Holy Spirit, God could not work amongst us. I also found it difficult living next door to the church. Our house and the church were in the same building block. When the church was closed, my front door became the front door of the church, and the pressure was immense. These two pressures were really getting me down, so I decided to spend some quality time with the Lord in prayer.

Often, when I needed to be alone with the Lord, I would walk along the towpath of the Regents canal, quite close to the church, which runs for miles through the centre of London. On this occasion I did just that, and I asked the Lord to lead me in the way that He desired. I told Him that it was not easy living next door to the church in the centre of the city, and if possible, I would like to live somewhere else. I made it quite clear that I was finding the ministry difficult and some of the leadership intransigent when it came to change. I said a lot more and generally cried out to the Lord for help.

When I returned home I picked up a daily readings book, which I often used. The Bible passage for the day was from the book of Esther in the Old Testament. In the passage, Mordecai gives Queen Esther a very strong word about her obligation to help save the Jewish minority from persecution, because of her own Jewish ethnicity, and her obvious influence with her husband the King. The powerful challenge brought by Mordecai is found in Esther 4:14:

> "And who knows but that you have come to royal position for such a time as this." (NIV)

The short word, after the Bible verse, was entitled "God's Perfect Timing," and the author started by asking the reader whether he or she had considered the possibility that God had placed them in their present situation for a very definite purpose. He continued by describing my position exactly. My situation had become very difficult and tense, and there were times when I would rather have been anywhere else than where I was at that particular time. Because of this predicament, I was praying earnestly to God to either change my situation or solve my problems.

This extraordinary direct word continued. The author suggested that if my prayers were not answered in the way I desired, possibly God had purposely put me in that place and that situation so that I could influence or change it for the better through the Holy Spirit. He then made it quite clear that escapism was never the solution to the problem. He went on to stress that this was no time for defeat or surrender, but rather a time to ask God what He expected me to do in the situation, and then to be sensitive to the guidance of the Holy Spirit.

I knew without a doubt that God was talking to me. I had been crying out to Him, and He was powerfully answering my cry for help. As a result I stayed at the church at King's Cross, and we continued to live in the house next door to the church. God, in His own time, began to put right the things that had been wrong. He helped me to lead the people in the direction that He wanted us to go. Sadly one or two left, but many more came and joined us as we sought to be a witness for Jesus in the area.

Once again I have to ask the question, how did that happen? Why had the Almighty God, who oversees the smooth running of the whole universe, the time or the interest to deal with my problems? I am one very insignificant individual in a world population of seven billion, and God took time to answer my prayer for help in detail. Some would say that it was just chance that I picked up that particular readings book, which answered my questions in such an extraordinary manner, and gave me a solution to my problems, immediately after I had cried out to the Lord for help. Perhaps I would agree with them, if it did not happen time and time again.

CHAPTER NINETEEN

The nations of the earth have gathered

Over the years, our church gradually became more and more multicultural. This did not happen overnight, but we moved from seven or eight nationalities to about thirty five national groups which represented all five populated continents of the earth. It may be useful to briefly recall how that happened.

When we first arrived at the Church, my daughter Jennifer was studying at the London School of Theology. For the first two years she had lodged privately in the area where the college is located. But when we moved into ministry in London she decided to join us at King's Cross, and soon became involved in the ministry. The church building is next door to a small university campus and in close proximity to a number of student residential blocks. One or two students attended the church, but with the vast population of university students studying and living in the city, and the close proximity of many to our church building, it seemed to me that students were an obvious group to evangelize.

As we approached the beginning of the new academic year, I prepared a simple leaflet advertising our church programme, and distributed copies to various student bodies. My daughter Jennifer and I agreed to respond appropriately if any students arrived at our Sunday services. To our immense joy, about six students arrived at the first Sunday morning service of the new academic year. That morning I announced that we would be having a student fellowship meeting on the Wednesday evening, and that Jennifer Smith, my daughter, was our student worker. I asked Jennifer to stand, and introduced her to those present. This was the beginning of a very successful student ministry. As the numbers grew, I realized that we needed a full time student worker. To cut a very long story short, and it is a long story, I successfully lobbied for a grant from the Baptist Union of Great Britain and the London Baptist Association, to support a full time student worker. Consequently, about four years after our arrival at the church we took on our first full time student worker, and he is still doing an excellent job today.

Some time before this I had met a young man from the Congo, who was attending a French wedding, held in our building, by a French speaking church. He introduced himself to me and told me that he was a Baptist. He said he was attending the French speaking church as his ability in the English language was limited. However, he assured me that once his English improved he would join our church, and this he did some time later. A short time after his arrival he told me about a dream that he had. In this dream, he met a white man who helped him become a minister of the Gospel in London. He then went on to say that I was that man. Nine years later that same young man is a fully qualified pastor, working on the staff of the church, running a French speaking congregation which draws its attendees mostly from the Franco African immigrant population of London.

CHAPTER TWENTY

What about the Indigenous people of the United Kingdom?

There is no doubt that the King's Cross Baptist Church has been really blessed because it is so multinational, but that has not stopped me asking the Lord what He is going to do about the indigenous people of the United Kingdom. One of the reasons why the average church attendance in London is higher than any other city in the United Kingdom is because the percentage of the population which is immigrant is higher than any other city in the land. Simply put, church attendance is boosted by keen Christians from all over the world, who have now settled in London.

When I first felt called to London, I envisaged preaching the Gospel to all those who would listen, but I imagined that my audience would include a majority of indigenous British people – that, however, has not been my experience. At times I have felt a little bit like the Apostle Paul, who recognized that God was using him to bring Gentiles to know Jesus as Lord and Saviour, but also expressed a longing to see his own people, the Jews, come to accept Jesus as their Messiah.

On one occasion I was sitting in a prayer meeting in our church, which was being led by one of the other leaders, and I asked the Lord to show me what our ministry direction should be in London. I immediately felt Him instruct me to turn to Genesis 12:3 where I read how God called Abraham and promised Him that:

"All people on earth will be blessed through you."
(NIV)

My immediate response was that I knew the passage very well, and I realized that our ministry in the centre of London was to reach the people of the earth. But I was not satisfied, so I asked the Lord to give me further clarification from the New Testament. Immediately I felt the Lord tell me to look at Galatians 3:7-8, and this is what I read:

"The scripture foresaw that God would justify the Gentiles by faith, and announced the Gospel in advance to Abraham: 'All nations will be blessed through you.'" (NIV)

So that was quite clear then, God wanted us to take the incredible opportunity afforded by our strategic position in the centre of the city of London, to reach every tribe and nation with the Gospel of Jesus. As I have already mentioned, I did know the Genesis passage well, and when God directed me to that passage, I knew what I was going to read before I read it. But I have to confess that, at the time, even though I knew the contents of Galatians reasonably well, I had no idea that God was about to direct me to Paul's report on the very verse I had just read in Genesis. Naturally, I readily accepted God's Word to me about our ministry being to the nations of the earth, but I did remind the Lord that the indigenous people of the United Kingdom are also amongst the nations of the earth. I am pleased to report that we saw them, as well as those from other countries, coming to know Jesus as Lord and Saviour and getting baptized.

CHAPTER TWENTY ONE

What about my family?

Like many people who serve the Lord full time, I did not spend enough time with the members of my own family, particularly in their early years. Because of this omission, I now spend a lot of time trying to put right the wrongs of the past, both personally and in prayer. Some time ago I was praying for two particular members of my family, and in my prayer I asked the Lord to either give them Christian friends, or to give them friends who would become interested in Christian things. To my surprise, the following Sunday, one of the members I had prayed for arrived at Church with a friend. After church I asked him what it was that had encouraged him to attend, on that particular Sunday, and he responded by saying that his friend had approached him and had asked him if he knew of a good church, as he was feeling a need for God.

Now you have got to admit that that was quite extraordinary, but there is still more. They attended Church every Sunday for about six weeks and then stopped. Disappointed, I approached the family member in question, and asked him what had happened to bring their attendance to an end. His reply was that his friend had recently read Richard Dawkins' book "The God Delusion", which may have affected his interest in the things of God. I immediately protested that I could prove to him, and his friend, that God does exist. I went on to tell him how I had prayed for him, that God would either give him Christian friends, or friends who would become interested in Christian things, and the following week he and his friend, who had suddenly become interested in Christian things, attended church. "Surely", I said, "your friend was an answer to my prayer."

I think the family member in question was affected by the experience but not entirely convinced that God was involved. When I asked him how he responded to what had happened, he said that he just wanted someone outside of his family to tell him about these things. So I began to pray that someone outside the family would speak to him about God. Approximately two weeks later we received a call from him, he explained that he was calling because he had just had a rather strange experience. He had been standing with some friends on the south bank of the river Thames, near the various theatres, where thousands gather at the weekend to socialize at the pubs, cafes, and restaurants, when a girl approached him and said that she was on a treasure hunt, and that she thought that he may be her treasure. He immediately assumed, correctly, that she was from a church, and engaged her in conversation. After a minute or two a young man arrived and joined in the conversation. He was more direct in his approach and said that he had a word from God for him. "You are an actor", he said, "and at the moment you are not getting the parts for which you have auditioned. The fact that some of your friends are getting work and you are not, fills you with disappointment, but don't worry, God is not finished with you yet." Apparently, "the word from God" pretty much summed up his situation. Once again my prayers had been answered. God had used someone outside of the family to speak to him about His existence and His desire to have a relationship with all those that He has created.

The question is, how did that happen? On two occasions specific prayers for action by God were answered in detail, the first time within a week, and the second time within two weeks. Was that just chance? I think that you have to agree that it was not. What is more, how did the man, with a word of knowledge, know all about this person who he had never met before, nor heard about? From where did he get that revelation if God is just a delusion?

CHAPTER TWENTY TWO

Does God ever defy science when
He answers our prayers?

There is no doubt that the New Testament makes it quite clear that we should expect answers to prayer which defy that which is natural. Our Lord Jesus encouraged His disciples to expect God to work supernaturally through them. In the three years that He spent with them, He taught them by what He said and what He did, that God works in and through those who have surrendered their lives to Him. In John chapters 13 to 16 Jesus prepared them for His departure, this included an explanation of His relationship with God the Father and God the Holy Spirit. He made it quite clear that, although He was going to leave them to go to His Father, He would still be with them because His Holy Spirit would indwell them. He went on to explain how the indwelling Holy Spirit would enable them to carry on Jesus' ministry to the point that they would be able to do the things that He had done. In John 14:12 -13 Jesus said:

> "I tell you the truth, anyone who has faith in me will do what I have been doing. He will do even greater things than these, because I am going to the Father. And I will do whatever you ask in my name, so that the Son may bring glory to the Father." (NIV)

Now it is important for us to realise that Jesus was not giving His followers the freedom to ask and to do whatever they desired, He was giving them the power to do whatever He desired. Our purpose is not to bring glory to ourselves; our purpose, like Jesus' purpose, is to "bring glory to the Father." The New Testament makes it quite clear that those who followed Jesus were used by God, in the power of His Holy Spirit, to heal the sick and to make the blind see, and in so doing they defied science. The writer to the Hebrews says in Hebrews 11:6:

> "And without faith it is impossible to please God, because anyone who comes to Him must believe that He exists and that He rewards those who earnestly seek Him." (NIV)

When Jesus spoke about faith, He was talking about ongoing faith – that is, faith which starts at the point of salvation and proceeds on into a life of faith. Earlier in this book, I referred to Mark 5:21-43 with specific reference to the woman who was healed from her chronic bleeding, when she touched the hem of Jesus' garment. But in this passage we have two extraordinary miracles. In addition to the healing of the woman who suffered from chronic bleeding, we have a young girl raised from the dead by Jesus.

Jesus had been having a busy day, so He crossed over to the other side of the lake, possibly to get a little rest. But when He got there He found a large crowd waiting for Him, hoping for more excitement from this extraordinary teacher and worker of miracles. Shortly after His arrival a man by the name of Jairus, who was a ruler in the local synagogue, fell on his knees before Jesus and pleaded with Him to save his daughter who was dying. The gospel writer, Mark, says that Jesus went with him. But just at that point the woman with the chronic bleeding problem arrived at the scene. Unfortunately, she stopped the Lord going with Jairus to help his daughter. After she was healed, Jesus ministered to her, so that she would understand who it was who had healed her.

Jairus must have been very concerned about his daughter's worsening condition, and when he saw his servants coming down the lane, he knew the worst had happened. Their message to him was that he need not bother the teacher any longer as his daughter was dead. He must have been devastated. If only the woman had not taken up the teacher's time, things could have been different. But in the midst of His devastation, Jesus makes an extraordinary statement. Mark 5:36:

> "Ignoring what they said, Jesus told the synagogue ruler, 'don't be afraid; just believe.'" (NIV)

There are two steps to faith, and both of them are included in our Lord's statement. Firstly we need to ignore the sceptics. The writer tells us that Jesus ignored what the man's servants said. A little later on when the mourners at the house, where the little girl lay dead, laughed at His statement that she was only asleep, Jesus had them put outside the house. So we need to ignore the sceptics, and then secondly, simply believe that the Almighty God can do anything. Nothing is too difficult for God, and He has your best at heart.

On another occasion when Jesus was talking about the power of faith, He said in Mark 11:22-24:

> "Have faith in God... I tell you the truth, if anyone says to this mountain, 'Go throw yourself into the sea,' and does not doubt in his heart but believes that what he says will happen, it will be done for him. Therefore I tell you, whatever you ask for in prayer, believe that you have received it, and it will be yours." (NIV)

Once again we need to understand that Jesus was talking about asking the Father to do that which is within His will and purpose. I refer you again to 1 John 5:14-15:

> "This is the confidence we have in approaching God:
> that if we ask anything according to His will, He hears
> us. And if we know that He hears us – whatever we
> ask – we know that we have what we asked of Him."
> (NIV)

So Jesus got rid of the mourners because their lack of faith in
Him would have had a negative effect on the miraculous
being done in the house of Jairus. Mark, speaking in the
following chapter, says that Jesus was not able to do many
miracles in His home town of Nazareth because of their
unbelief. So after getting rid of the sceptics Jesus went to the
little girl's beside and ministered to her. Mark 5:41-42:

> "He took her by the hand and said to her, 'Talitha
> koum!' (Which means, 'little girl, I say to you, get
> up!'). Immediately the girl stood up and walked
> around (she was twelve years old). At this they were
> completely astonished." (NIV)

What an extraordinary thing to happen, yet nothing has
changed in our day. Many who today claim to be believers,
would have been put out by the Lord for their unbelief,
because they don't really believe that God is able to do the
miraculous in the 21st century. Genuine Christian faith trusts
in a God who can overcome the problems of life and
accomplish His purpose in our day, just as He did in biblical
times.

You will notice that I did not say take away the problems
of life. Sometimes God does miraculously take away the
problems of life, by healing our sickness, or removing the
obstacle in our way, or delivering us from whatever is
oppressing us. But on other occasions he gives us the grace
and strength to overcome the problems of life, or to live
through them, and when at last they are over we know that

we are a stronger person and a much more mature Christian. The Apostle Paul asked God to take away what he described in 2 Corinthians 12:7 as "a thorn in my flesh, a messenger of Satan, to torment me." (NIV) And he tells us how God responded in verses 8-9:

> "Three times I pleaded with the Lord to take it away from me. But He said to me, 'My grace is sufficient for you, for my power is made perfect in weakness.' Therefore I will boast all the more gladly about my weakness, so that Christ's power may rest on me." NIV

We don't always know why God allows one difficult experience and then delivers us from another. Why, for example, in my opening anecdote at the beginning of this book, did God allow my friend's business to fall into unprofitability, and then miraculously direct me in answer to his wife's prayer, to arrive at the crucial moment to minister to him in his time of need? Quite simply, we must accept that God knows all things, and there are times when God will take us out of a situation, even a business, because He does not want us to be doing what we are doing. He has other plans for us. The fact is, we need to get our priorities right. Just look at Jesus' profound statement In Matthew 6:31-33:

> "So do not worry, saying, 'What shall we eat?' or 'What shall we wear?' For the pagans run after all these things, and your heavenly Father knows that you need them. But seek first his kingdom and his righteousness, and all these things will be given to you as well." (NIV)

Mankind's problem is that we spend most of our time seeking after all the things of life, then when we find ourselves in trouble we cry out to God, asking Him to help us in our time of need. So our Lord Jesus, in His sermon on the mount, encouraged all of us who wish to follow Him, to give God the leadership of our lives, and to live in accordance with His understanding of right and wrong, then He will make sure that all the things that we need to live this life to the full, will be ours as well. That's what Jesus meant when He said: "But seek first His kingdom and his righteousness, and all these things will be given to you as well". (Matthew 6:33, NIV). However, there have been times in my life when I have become angry with the evil one, because he will not stop attacking those who are trying to get it right.

CHAPTER TWENTY THREE

How do we overcome the audacity of the Evil One?

I would like to go back for a moment to our ministry in South Africa. A mother and her three children started attending one of our Durban congregations. Within the first few weeks of attendance she committed her life to the Lord, and her children became involved in the appropriate departments of the church. Their commitment, as a family, to the life of the church, was developing very nicely when the mother told us that she had some bad news. Her eldest daughter had been experiencing some pain, and upon investigation it was discovered that she had ovarian cancer. At first I was shocked that such a young girl could be afflicted in this way, she was nearly sixteen but looked about fourteen. My second reaction was anger with the audacity of the evil one. Just when this little family were getting things right, he could not resist stepping in to mess things up.

My first response was to get the leadership together and to pray earnestly for her healing. Some of the leaders prayed that God would guide her doctors, but one particular brother prayed that God would heal her. The following week I visited the family in their home, and the sick daughter was in bed, so I sat next to her bed and talked to her about Jesus. I asked her if she had personally asked Jesus to come into her life, and she said that she had not. I then asked her if she would like to do that, and she responded positively. After we had finished praying for her salvation, I prayed again for her healing and encouraged her to trust Jesus who had saved her from her sin, to also heal her from her cancer.

A short while after my visit, her mother took her back to hospital to investigate the progress of her cancer. The doctor was astonished to discover that the growth had decreased in size without any medical treatment, and it continued to do so until it disappeared completely. The question is, how did this happen? The answer is, our God is an amazing God who not only defeated the evil one when He rose from the dead on Easter Sunday, but continually defeats the work of the evil one in the lives of those who trust Him absolutely. Salvation is an ongoing experience. It starts when we first receive Jesus as our Lord and Saviour, and goes on through our lives as we experience His saving grace in our day to day living. Jesus encouraged His followers to pray the prayer that we now call the "Lord's prayer", found in its most complete form in Matthew 6:9-13. In verse 13 Jesus concludes the prayer by saying:

> "And lead us not into temptation, but deliver us from the evil one." (NIV)

My response to this part of our Lord's prayer is, if the Saviour of the world taught His followers to continually ask God the Father to deliver us from the evil one, surely we should expect our God to respond positively to such a request, and deliverance from the evil one must include the healing of sickness that he brings upon us. As Christians we were never meant to live defeated lives, continually being the victims of the devil himself. God always intended for us to live in victory. The Apostle Paul, describing the Christian's experience in his letter to the Roman church, said this in Romans 8:28 & 31-35 & 37-39:

> "And we know that in all things God works for the good of those who love him, who have been called according to his purpose... What, then, shall we say

in response to this? If God is for us, who can be against us? He who did not spare his own Son, but gave him up for us all – how will he not also, along with him, graciously give us all things? Who will bring any charge against those who God has chosen? It is God who justifies. Who is he that condemns? Christ Jesus, who died – more than that, who was raised to life – is at the right hand of God and is also interceding for us. Who shall separate us from the love of Christ? Shall trouble or hardship or persecution or famine or nakedness or danger or sword? No, in all these things we are more than conquerors through him who loved us. For I am convinced that neither death nor life, nether angels nor demons, neither the present nor the future, nor any powers, neither height nor depth, nor anything else in all creation, will be able to separate us from the love of God that is in Christ Jesus our Lord." (NIV)

In actual fact the devil is not particularly concerned about defeated Christians, those who are just an audience, who listen to the Word of God but never do anything. He is, however, concerned about those who are applying the Word of God to their lives – those who are actively living for Jesus. The Apostle Peter exhorts his readers in 1 Peter 5:8-10:

"Be self-controlled and alert. Your enemy the devil prowls around like a roaring lion looking for someone to devour. Resist him, standing firm in the faith, because you know that your brothers throughout the world are undergoing the same kind of suffering. And the God of all grace, who called you to his eternal glory in Christ, after you have suffered a little while, will himself restore you and make you strong, firm and steadfast." (NIV)

Peter makes it very clear that all those who seek to accomplish God's purpose for their lives, will be attacked by the evil one. But he also encourages them to resist the devil and stand firm in their faith, because our God, who works out our salvation perfectly, is not going to let us down in our spiritual battles with the evil one. We just need to stand firm, trusting Him completely to overcome the evil one for us. Because, as Paul said in Romans 8:28, we know that God is working for the good of those who love Him, and are seeking to accomplish His purpose. If we allow Him to fight our battles through us, He has promised us that we will win, because He is God and He loves us.

Our big God is interested in our small needs

The postal code for The King's Cross Baptist Church is WC1X 9EW; the first three digits stand for West Central One, which indicates a very central position in the City of London. That central position and the close proximity of the Church to excellent transport links meant that we often had visitors from other parts of the United Kingdom or from overseas. Some years back, a group representing a number of Baptist churches from the United States of America started using the building as a launch pad to prayer walk the city centre. About every six months they would arrive with a team, some of whom had been before and some who had not. After using the church building a few times, they asked if I would be willing to participate in the induction of their new team members by giving a talk on London and what our church was doing in the city to advance the Gospel. Quite naturally some of the team started to attend the church when they were visiting, and one thing led to another, and we became friends.

During one of these visits, one of their leaders, a pastor in his church in the USA, asked if our church would be interested in forming a relationship with their church in Birmingham, Alabama. They said that they were interested in our church because we were very multicultural, which they said was something that they could learn from us. They went on to ask if I would like to attend a missions conference at their church in the USA where I could share with their congregation what we were doing in London. Now, I have to confess that I enjoyed their company while they were in London, but I was not sure that I was meant to form a more formal relationship with them, so I decided to pray about it. My prayer was rather negative as I was trying to persuade the Lord to tell me not to go, but He did just the opposite. Asking the Lord for a word, I picked up a daily readings book and opened it at the appropriate date. I can't remember the exact biblical verse, but it was an exhortation for believers to have fellowship with one another. The commentator then pointed out the need for churches to relate to one another and encouraged leaders of churches to seek relationships with other churches, especially those from other countries. God spoke to me very directly, and I had no doubt that he wanted me to go to the Missions conference in Birmingham, Alabama.

Contrary to all my expectations, we had a wonderful time in the USA. I thought I was going there to tell them how to run a multicultural church, but as it turned out, they had so much to teach me. I returned home with all kinds of new ideas and a new desire to do things with excellence. I trust that they, too, were blessed in the process. This all happened because the Lord was interested in what I would have considered a minor detail of my life. God longs to lead us in those areas that we are inclined to dismiss as too small for His attention, but it is often the little details that lead to big changes in our Christian experience.

CHAPTER TWENTY FIVE

God's timing is perfect

I mentioned earlier that my parents' last posting in full time ministry was to a small town in northern Natal, South Africa. They spent ten extraordinary years between the ages of 68 and 78, redeveloping a badly declined ministry. During this period, I often spoke to my father about when he would finally bring his full time ministry to an end. It was always rather difficult to mention the word "retire," which was not really part of his vocabulary. In fact, he had made little or no preparation for such an event. However, in his 78th year I encouraged him to apply for a flat in a large retirement home in Durban, not far from where we were living at the time. He responded in a predictable fashion and did not show much enthusiasm. When I explained that it was just a speculative application which might not yield much initially, he agreed to fill in the relevant forms.

When the completed forms arrived by post, I took them to the management of the retirement centre, and the gentleman to whom I gave them began to read them in my presence. He immediately showed a keen interest in the content, because he discovered that my father was both an ordained minister and a wounded veteran from the Second World War. He explained that as a board member of another organization, which looked after war veterans, he would like my father to fill in another set of forms. As you can imagine, getting my father to fill in the second set of forms was no easier than getting him to fill in the first set. But he did, and they too were returned to the gentleman who had shown such an interest in him. To my surprise this same gentleman phoned me just three weeks later, and he asked me if I thought my parents would be willing to retire by the end of the following month because one of their new cottages, inexplicably, had not been taken by anyone on the waiting list. I told him that it may take a bit longer than one month, as my father would need to give his Church notice of his intention to retire, and the man was happy to wait. Amazingly Dad and Mom agreed to retire, and within three months they were settled in their beautiful new cottage, just down the road from where I was living with my family.

There were a number of reasons why my father had agreed to retire from full time ministry, but the most significant reason was that the timing was perfect. Sometime after my parents moved into their cottage, my father and I had a good talk about things. He told me that just before I had phoned about their possible retirement, there had been a very difficult problem with one of the members of the church, and when this had occurred, he had for the first time in his life thought, that perhaps it was the right time to retire. He confessed to me that after this incident he had felt quite depressed, which was not like him at all. Then one morning a woman, whom he had never met before, phoned him and asked if he was the Rev. George Smith. She went on to say that she read his newspaper column every week, and although she had never met him, she had seen his picture in the news paper, and she felt as if she knew him. She then gave Dad a word from the Lord. She told him that he was one of God's choice servants, and that God loved him and was blessed by the work that he had done. My father was much encouraged by her word, but he also knew it was time to retire.

Once again we have to ask the question, how did this happen? Were these all chance occurrences or was God in it all? I choose to believe that God was in it all. For the next few years my father ministered in my church as the pastor for seniors, and we built up a closer relationship than we ever had before. He became the sounding board for many of my ideas, one of which I recalled earlier in this book.

CHAPTER TWENTY SIX

Is our experience anything like the New Testament?

It's easy to look at the New Testament and conclude that our Christian life does not bear much resemblance to the lives that God's servants lived in the early church. They seemed to experience miracles of God's deliverance and power all the time and, quite simply, we don't. But there are a number of things we need to take into account.

Firstly, it's important to recognize that the New Testament covers many years. To understand how many, we need to look at the probable date of the writing of the last book in the Bible. Revelation, as far as we know, was written towards the close of Emperor Domitian's reign in AD 96, sixty-three years after the death of our Lord Jesus. The account that we have before us represents the highs and the lows of the followers of Jesus over a considerable period of time, and over a large geographical area. In between the anecdotal evidence presented to us there were periods when the church ticked over without much to report, just as it does today.

However, we also need to recognize that in the New Testament we have a record of God working in and through the followers of Jesus in an extraordinary way, which often cuts right across that which is considered to be natural. God breaks the laws of science, showing quite clearly that these occurrences cannot be attributed to chance, but are in fact acts of the Almighty. In addition, we have to accept that God has not changed; He is just as able today to do the things He did two thousand years ago to accomplish His purpose. All He needs are willing followers who have received His salvation through Jesus, who have been filled with His Holy Spirit and trust Him implicitly. We have contemporary testimony from all kinds of sources that God is at work in the lives of His followers all over the world, defeating the evil one and supporting His ongoing purpose. The question is, are you willing to trust Him enough to move from being an onlooker to being one who is experiencing God's power in such a way that it affects those in your sphere of influence for good?

CHAPTER TWENTY SEVEN

Going back to the beginning

There are those, who, when questioned about their beliefs, will automatically lay claim to the religion or denomination of their parents. If their parents are Christian, and their denomination is Anglican, they too will claim to be Anglican even if they are not living the Christian life. In the United Kingdom more than 60% of the population claim to be Christian, but only 7% of the population actually attend church on a regular basis. Let me hasten to add that church attendance does not necessarily mean that you have a living faith in the Lord Jesus. Nor does a lack of church attendance necessarily mean that you are without faith. However, as the New Testament urges us not to neglect gathering together as believers on a regular basis, one has to question what has happened to those who no longer meet together with their brothers and sisters in the Lord, to worship the Almighty God, as the body of Christ.

My experience could have been identical to those who, for convenience sake, claim the religion or denomination of their parents – but have no living faith. But what would be the purpose if I did not really believe? As I have already explained, my parents emigrated from the United Kingdom in 1949 to what was then Rhodesia to serve as missionaries. When I was about six years old, we lived in a block of flats in the centre of Ndola, Northern Rhodesia now Zambia. I shared a bedroom with my brother Brian who was two years older than me. One night, after lights out, we were talking quietly in the dark when he suddenly asked me a very important question, "Andrew, are you a Christian?" I replied indignantly, "Of course I am a Christian. Mom and Dad are Christians and they are missionaries, so I am a Christian!" My eight year old brother then explained, with some maturity, considering his age, that everyone has to make their own commitment to follow Jesus. His explanation obviously impressed me because I said that I would do that quietly on my own. I can't remember the exact words I said, but that night I prayed, and in my prayer I told Jesus that I wanted to follow Him, and that I wanted Him to be my Saviour.

In many ways my first commitment to follow Jesus was very childish, I was after all only six years old, but I have no doubt it was real, and that the Lord God Almighty took me seriously. I know that in the years that followed I did things that grieved Him, but I can tell you today that I have loved the Lord God, and His Son Jesus, my Saviour, for as long as I can remember.

My next spiritual experience of significance came a few years later. I was about thirteen when an evangelist by the name of Richard Green arrived from South Africa to hold a series of meetings in our area, which included the Ndola Baptist Church. I remember as a young lad being riveted by his preaching at a Sunday evening meeting. He spoke about the Cross of Calvary, and he explained how Jesus, the Son of God, had given up all His godly privileges to come and live as a man on earth, with all the limitations that we have, and then to die a truly agonizing death, in our place, on a wooden cross. He explained how all of us – men women and children – have sinned against God; that is, we have broken God's perfect law by the way we live our lives and consequently have received the penalty of death for our sin. However, God loves the world so much that He sent His Son Jesus to die in our place so that we may be forgiven. The climax of the evangelist's presentation was the resurrection of Jesus, who overcame death and sin and Hell on our behalf so that we may be forgiven and receive eternal life.

At the end of this really powerful presentation, he made an appeal for all those who wanted to receive God's forgiveness and salvation, to go forward to the front of the church. I was so grateful that Jesus had died in my place, and I desperately wanted to go forward, but I could not, because Mom and Dad were missionaries. What would people think? However, when I went out of the church that evening, I certainly accepted God's forgiveness for my sin. I looked up to Heaven and said, "Lord Jesus, I love you with all my heart and I will serve you forever." My promise was real, and God knew that I meant business, and He has enabled me to live for Him for many years since then.

The third and last spiritual experience which has shaped my Christian life happened many years later. Having ministered in my first church in East London, South Africa, for a few years, I was invited to be the associate pastor of a considerably larger church in Cape Town. I believed the call to be of God and moved to Cape Town to take up a very different ministry to the one I was leaving. After a short period of time in the new ministry, the other pastor informed me that he would be taking a three month, overseas, sabbatical break. Naturally, as the associate pastor I was expected to lead the church of about 300 people while he was away. I have to confess that I was mildly apprehensive by the prospect. Unlike my previous church, which had been mainly frequented by suburban families, my new church attracted a lot of university students and some academics, amongst whom was the principal of a local theological college who was also a prominent leader in our church. I felt that my own training was rather humble by comparison to theirs, and I was concerned that I would not make the grade. However, I need not have worried because God's plan was going ahead perfectly.

At the time of my crisis a Christian film was doing the rounds which told the story of a well known nineteenth century missionary to China. In the film the narrator spoke of a time when the missionary came to a "cross-roads" in his Christian experience. Recognizing that he needed an outpouring of God's Holy Spirit in his life to enable him to accomplish what God had set before him, he decided to spend some time alone with God. He particularly desired more compassion and love for the lost, and a fresh understanding of their need to be saved. God powerfully responded to his cry for help, completely transforming his ministry and equipping him to do the work that the Lord had set before him.

We showed the film in our church on a Sunday evening. I went on my own because my wife Muriel had stayed at home to look after our six month old triplets and four year old son. I remember watching the film and being deeply moved by the missionaries' experience. After it was all over, I went outside and sat in my car in the car park, and there I cried out to God, telling Him that I needed that same outpouring of His Holy Spirit that the missionary had experienced so that I could accomplish the job that He had set before me. God knew that I really meant it, because He came down on me in power. I have never in my life had such an extraordinary experience before or since. The presence of God was so powerfully upon me that I could feel Him touching my life with His Holy Spirit. But I needed to get home, my wife Muriel would be wondering where I was, so I drove home with difficulty.

When I arrived home, through my tears, I tried to explain to Muriel what was happening to me, but as you can imagine it was not easy. So I took the dog for a walk around the streets, and all the time I could feel the extraordinary presence of God. I do not know how long this went on for, but I do

know that God was doing something powerful in my life.
I finally went to bed and woke up the next morning feeling
like a new man. I realized that I was much more aware of His
presence and purpose, and His direction for my life, and I
really wanted to get on with running the church that He had
given me to lead.

My fellow pastor had already gone on his three month
sabbatical and I was preaching at most of the services. After
this experience God led me to preach from the beginning of
Acts, where Peter addressed the crowd at Pentecost, following
the mighty outpouring of God's Holy Spirit on the followers
of Jesus. Acts 2:38 says:

> "Peter replied, 'Repent and be baptized, everyone of
> you, in the name of Jesus Christ for the forgiveness of
> sins. And you will receive the gift of the Holy Spirit.'"
> (NIV)

The first Sunday I preached on the need for repentance before
salvation could happen in the life of the individual. I told the
congregation that it is not enough to want salvation. It is not
even enough to put our faith in the death and resurrection of
Jesus to save us. We need also to repent, that is, to turn away
from our past lives of sin, and in the power of the Holy Spirit
seek to live our lives according to God's perfect standard.
I finished the presentation with an appeal for those who were
willing to repent and put their faith in Jesus for forgiveness
and salvation, to come to the front of the church, and a small
number of people responded.

The second Sunday, I preached on Baptism. I made it
quite clear that Jesus' teaching and example required that
those who were truly "born again" spiritually, needed to be
baptized by immersion in obedience to our Lord's command
in Matthew 28:18-20. I emphasized the need for a public
declaration of faith. I used Romans 6:1-6 to show that

immersion, that is, going under the water and coming up again, quite clearly portrays the death, burial and resurrection of the Lord Jesus, who paid the price for our sin. In verse 4 of that chapter Paul says:

> "We were therefore buried with Him through baptism into death in order that, just as Christ was raised from the dead through the glory of the Father, we too may live a new life." (NIV)

Once again I made an appeal and a number of people came to the front of the church to declare their need for baptism.

Then on the third Sunday, I knew that I had to preach on being filled with the Holy Spirit. I also knew that I would have opposition from one or two of the leaders of the church, because being filled with the Holy Spirit is part of the Christian experience that has been interpreted in different ways by different groups in the church. Sitting in my study one day, I began to think about how God wanted me to approach the subject. I envisaged the front of the church, and saw myself making an appeal for those who wanted to be filled with the Holy Spirit to come to the front of the church. In my vision the response was phenomenal. At least a quarter of the congregation of about two hundred and fifty people responded positively. I was quite overwhelmed by what I saw, and was still thinking about it when a young man knocked at my door. The young man in question was a very keen Christian, and for some reason I could not stop myself telling him what I had just seen, and to share with him my hesitation about preaching on the subject. He, in turn, responded by encouraging me to be obedient to the Lord and to preach on what God had given me.

After he left, I chastised myself for telling him what had happened to me. I realized that, having told someone, I could no longer back down. I would have to preach on the subject and trust that God would do the rest. In hindsight, I am sure that God sent my visitor to keep me in line with His purpose.

That Sunday, in obedience to God's direction, I preached on being filled with the Holy Spirit, so that we may be equipped to serve God with the power that He alone can give. I concluded the sermon by telling them what had happened to me just a few weeks earlier. After the sermon, I made an appeal for those who wanted to be filled with God's Holy Spirit to come forward. To my astonishment, that which I saw in my vision happened exactly. A quarter of the congregation came forward for ministry – there was not enough room for them at the front, and the aisles began to fill up as well. I was quite overcome and did not really know what I should do next. Eventually we took the whole group of people to another hall appropriately known as the "upper room." Prayer and ministry went on for a long time and many people were touched by God in a fresh and powerful way.

In the New Testament, the disciples of Jesus went through many spiritual experiences after they first put their faith in Jesus for salvation and forgiveness. They soon realised that it was easy to dry up spiritually, and the only way to remedy that dryness was to be filled with the Holy Spirit again. I find it interesting that the same followers of Jesus, who were filled with the Holy Spirit at Pentecost, in Acts 2, were filled with the Holy Spirit again in Acts 4. The religious authorities had arrested Peter and John for preaching in the name of Jesus, and kept them in prison overnight. Then, before releasing them, they commanded them to stop speaking any longer in the name of Jesus. But the disciples were not deterred as we see in Acts 4:19-20:

> "But Peter and John replied, 'Judge for yourselves whether it is right in God's sight to obey you rather than God. For we cannot help speaking about what we have seen and heard.'" (NIV)

After their release they reported back to God's people where there was an explosion of prayer, praise, and prophecy. Luke concludes his report by saying in verse 31:

> "After they prayed, the place where they were meeting was shaken. And they were all filled with the Holy Spirit and spoke the word of God boldly." (NIV)

And these were the same disciples who had been filled with the Holy Spirit at Pentecost. This does not mean that the Holy Spirit departs from those who are committed Christians, and then indwells them again. God the Holy Spirit is always with us. But it's easy, with the pressures of life, to become oblivious to His presence, and to rely again upon our human ingenuity. It is then that we need a fresh touch of God's Holy Spirit, new inspiration, more compassion, more power, so that we may be equipped to serve Him and accomplish His extraordinary purpose in His strength and not ours.

CHAPTER TWENTY EIGHT

Conclusion

I am sure you will realise by now that I cannot possibly agree with those who believe that God is a delusion, because the evidence for His existence is truly overwhelming. I find it very interesting that the atheist is only mentioned twice in the Bible, and on each occasion the writer says exactly the same thing, Psalm 14:1 and Psalm 53:1:

> "The fool says in his heart, 'There is no God.'" (NIV)

I also note with interest that Jesus, the Saviour of the world, offers salvation to everyone who will believe in Him, no one is excluded. In John 3:16-17 Jesus says:

> "For God so loved the world that he gave his one and only Son, that whoever believes in him shall not perish but have eternal life. For God did not send his Son into the world to condemn the world, but to save the world through him." (NIV)

God is filled with compassion for every person He has created. He longs for us to accept His way of salvation through Jesus.

Peter, one of Jesus disciples says in 2 Peter 3:9:

> "The Lord is not slow in keeping His promise, as some understand slowness. Instead he is patient with you, not wanting anyone to perish, but everyone to come to repentance." (NIV)

God's forgiveness and salvation are available because Jesus died in our place, paying the penalty for our sin, and then came alive again, defeating death and sin and Hell. But that is not all, He also enables us to live for Him by putting His Holy Spirit in us, so that we will know what His will is, and do it in His strength.

You may respond to what I have said by saying that there are many roads that lead to God, and you are following another road. But I urge you to consider Jesus' statement in John 14:6 where He says:

> "I am the way and the truth and the life. No one comes to the Father (that is Father God) except through me." (NIV)

There are two steps to salvation, Repentance and Faith.

Repentance:

Peter, preaching right after Pentecost said in Acts 3:19:

> "Repent then, and turn to God, so that your sins may be wiped out." (NIV)

The word, repent, means to change your mind, to recognize that the way you are living your life is the wrong way, and that Jesus way is the right way.

Faith:

The Apostle Paul said in Ephesians 2:8-9:

> "For it is by grace you have been saved, through faith – and this not from yourselves, it is the gift of God – not by works, so that no one can boast."

In other words, your good works cannot save you. God has made the way of salvation and it is completely free. Jesus, God the Son, died for your sin and then rose from the dead to overcome the devil, sin, and Hell. By faith you need to accept these facts, receive God's free forgiveness and put your life in His hands so that He may become your Lord and Saviour.

This is how you should pray:

"Dear Father God, thank you for providing a way to be saved. I am sorry for the things I have done wrong in my life. (If there is any particular sin on your conscience, confess that sin and ask God for His forgiveness.) Please forgive me. In faith I now turn from my way of living to your way of living. Thank you, Jesus, for dying on the cross in my place. I am so grateful that you overcame the devil's plan to destroy humanity, by rising from the dead. Please come into my life by your Holy Spirit. In faith I receive you now as my Lord and Saviour. Thank you for forgiveness and the gift of your Holy Spirit, in Jesus name, amen.

What happens next?

1. Tell someone

Start by telling someone you think will be pleased to hear the news.

2. Read the Bible

The Bible is God's message to us. We need to get to know more about what He has said.

3. Pray to God

We can talk to God the Father as a friend. We can do this because Jesus died to repair our relationship with Him.

4. Join a local church

Church is our spiritual family where together we worship God, hear what God is saying to us and encourage each other.

May God truly bless you as you follow Him through Jesus your Lord and Saviour.